MW00697902

THE HAPPY TEACHER'S HANDBOOK

From Overwhelmed to Inspired: Helping Teachers Embrace Resiliency

JEN MOLITOR

CONTENTS

Copyright © 2019 by Lift up Leaders, LLC
Jen Molitor
Published by Jen Molitor
www.happyteachershandbook.com

All rights reserved. No part of this publication may be reproduced, distributed, or transmitted in any form or by any means, including photocopying, recording, or other electronic or mechanical methods, without the prior written permission of the publisher, except in the case of brief quotations embodied in reviews and certain other non-commercial uses permitted by copyright law. The resource pages at the end of the book may be used by those who purchased the book.

Although the author and publisher have made every effort to ensure that the information in this book was correct at the time of publishing, the author and publisher do not assume and hereby disclaim any liability to any party for any loss, damage, or disruption caused by errors or omissions, whether such errors or omissions result from negligence, accident, or other cause.

The events and conversations in this book have been set down to the best of the author's ability, although some names and details have been changed to protect the privacy of individuals.

The advice and strategies found within may not be suitable for every situation. This work is sold with the understanding that neither the author nor the publisher are held responsible for the results accrued from the advice in this book.

First paperback edition July 2019
ISBN-13: 978-1-7331228-0-1 (paperback)

DEDICATION

This book is dedicated to all the students who have crossed my path.

You inspire me to be a better human and teacher.

And to Edwin and Cecelia - your imagination, curiosity, and compassion are the kindling to my flame of inspiration.

ACKNOWLEDGMENTS

Thank you to all those who encouraged me to write this book. Gus, for letting my time be consumed by writing and letting me continue chasing my dreams. Mom, for being my cheerleader and spontaneous editor. Dad, for believing in me.

Jess, for being my person - you are one phenomenal teacher and intuitive horse woman. Sean, for listening and encouraging. Thanks to both of you for letting me be your teacher each summer when we were younger.

Edwin and Cecelia, for giving up time with Mom so that I could finish this book and for contributing to so many of my life's lessons.

To all my colleagues in Mason, Ohio, where I started out on this teaching journey. We had so much fun planning, learning, and going on trips together. To my new colleagues in Clarksville, Ohio, for letting me try out new ideas, welcoming me into your teams, and putting up with "Jen 'Curb your Enthusiasm' Molitor." ☺ To the administrators for believing in me and who keep pushing me to continue growing.

Thank you to all my students. Thank you for challenging me to be a better teacher, for not being satisfied with the status quo, and for being thinkers. I see you. I hear you. I believe in you. Someday you will change the world.

FOREWORD

Teaching is intense. It mirrors raising your own children--exciting, frustrating, challenging, rewarding, impactful, arduous, and the most important and meaningful work there is! It is also just plain exhausting. Yet, the myths *still* exist. You know...Teachers only work six hours a day; they get summers off; taxpayers foot the bill for extensive benefits packages; teacher unions are not necessary; it is easy work--after all, they are only children. How tough could it be? Well, little do most know the everyday obstacles teachers graciously encounter. They take home countless tasks to grade on their nights and weekends; they spend hundreds of dollars of their own funds to ensure all students have supplies; they even bring extra snacks for students who need it. They counsel. They nurse. They parent. They comfort. They discipline. They mediate. They call a bluff. They get spat on and yelled at. They fight for those who need them, and they cry at night for those who have dire situations. In many instances, teachers provide second chances (and more) and, ultimately they save our humanity.

In this amazing resource, Jen opens our souls to the heart of the teaching profession. She humorously and eloquently writes what most teachers are thinking and experiencing. Jen reminds us to "start with the heart" (Chapter 1). *Do I matter? Do you see me? Am I worthy?* Jen highlights the needs of all students--all humans for that matter. Great teachers answer those questions for students on a regular basis by the implicit looks, the pats of confidence, and the time they take to truly ask, listen, and care.

This book will hook you with Jen's profound ability to tell you the story of teaching, as well as with the practical applications she suggests. Jen even tackles the ever-so-delicate topic of parent partnerships. As she articulates how you often feel after some bouts of parent communication, "You are fuming. Insulted. Disrespected. Offended" (Chapter 7). Yet, she poignantly reminded us to be kind. Always. And, she is absolutely right. We do not know others' stories. Jen uses *The 5 essential C's to parent partnerships*, and even shared a sample letter she sent to her students' parents. Jen does not stop there. She goes onto suggest her top five self-care strategies. You will love them!

As a lifelong educator, this resource is funny, interesting, and heartwarming. Enjoy!

—Dr. Tammy Heflebower

Author & Associate

Marzano Research Solution Tree

tammy.heflebower@marzanoresearch.com

@tammyhef

PREFACE

Teachers have amazing stories. Stories we share at the end of the day, when the halls are finally quiet. Stories of students letting the air out of bus tires to try and get school cancelled. Stories of 'that mom' who wore her hottie Santa outfit when she dropped off her son. The stories we tell our spouses and friends, ones that everyone insists we write down but never do.

As I traveled this past year, I decided to share some of these stories. Like this particular one about my own son who happened to be the topic of the crazy story of the day in my district. A colleague shared that some 3rd grade boys were complaining about one of the toilets being stopped up. She called the office to let them know, but suddenly another boy ran in saying that Edwin (my sweetpea) fixed it. Curiously, she headed to the hallway and saw Edwin walking back to class.

"Hey Edwin, I hear you fixed the toilet?"

"Yup," Edwin said sheepishly, staring at the ground and unsure if he was in trouble or not.

She casually said, "That's great! How'd you do it?"

He responded, "I just grabbed the paper towels and put them in the garbage."

She hoped she misunderstood. "Oh, you were cleaning up the floor, right?"

"No, I just grabbed the paper towels that were clogging the toilet. I didn't want the water to overflow."

Horrified, but seeing that he was truly just trying to help and a bit clueless about putting his hand in the toilet (I'm gagging a little as I type), she chatted with him about proper safety measures in the bathroom and sent him back to the restroom to scrub the heck out of his hands.

Unbelievable, right?! I wish it was.

Stories engage us. They make us cry, laugh, and in the case about the one with my son, they can make us gag. They also help us learn.

When you're finished with this book, you'll have a new-found desire to share more of your own stories. You'll also discover new strategies for unlocking the inspiration that's been wilted over the years due to being overwhelmed, the demands, and the pressure to grow all students.

To do our job well, to knock it out of the park, we need to find a way around the obstacles that will inevitably be in our paths. To be accomplished, with or without the prestige of a *Teacher of the Year* award, you've got to own it.

This handbook is your key. Take a deep breath. Sit up a little taller. Open your heart to new possibilities. Teaching is a gift, *your* gift to the world. Your transformation begins now.

"Someday I will change the world."

Your day is today.

INTRODUCTION

I'm teetering on the edge of a platform about 100 feet off the ground, attached to a nylon harness, wearing a helmet, and agonizing over my fear. My friends have sailed down the zipline laughing, cheering, and even doing dance moves in the air, as if those harnesses can really be trusted.

Not me. I'm terrified. I have a feeling it's going to be fun, safe, and exciting... but I just can't convince my fear to see it that way.

A polite, encouraging staff member asks if I want him to push me off the platform. Um, no.

My friends are cheering me on below, counting down... 3-2-1. And still I teeter.

Denise yells up to me.

"Jen, this place you're in right now represents other areas of your life when you were anxiously clinging to indecision. This place of suffering doesn't need to happen. Make a decision - you can jump or you can climb down. It doesn't matter. Just make a decision."

A little part of me thinks, "She thinks she knows me and understands this fear? She has no idea." A bigger part of me just wants to cry. Could there be truth to what she's saying?

I plead with the ropes holding me on to the zipline. "I want to do this. I can do this. I *should* do this."

I didn't understand my fear. Then, to add insult to injury, I judged myself for that fear and panic - how silly of me to be so scared. Perfect, now I had added embarrassment and guilt to the mix. I *could have* blamed that debilitating mix of fear, embarrassment, and guilt for interfering with my zipline adventure... But I realized there was only one thing standing in my way.

Me.

Another dear friend, Nurjahan (fear of heights introduced us), dropped down on the platform beside me.

"Jen, I'm terrified too. Watching you face your fear and persevere got me through this whole ropes course too. I'm going to sail down this zip line with you because I believe in you. I know you can do it. Can you do if for me too? I need you to."

She was actually benefiting from my fear, even as I sat feeling defeated and inadequate. But knowing it was up to me to make this decision, knowing I couldn't let Nurjahan down, I summoned up some courage.

By this time, quite a few of the staffers and my fellow teammates had gathered to see what was holding everyone up. They all counted, 3-2-1... I locked eyes with Nurjahan and we jumped (well, I just teetered the rest of the way off the platform), screamed, and held on to the rope for dear life.

And, I made it. Safely. And.... it might have been a little fun - at the very end, when I knew I was alive.

I learned quite a lot during the UCSD Challenge Course. While learning the technicalities of navigating a ropes course is on that list, the realizations I made about myself were far more powerful.

Fear is insightful. It's a window that we sometimes allow to become our windshield, a lens for choosing our path in life. Through that lens, we make decisions about what we avoid and what we pursue. While fear-based decisions can be supportive if used correctly, fully living our life through that lens can keep us from reaching our goals.

Fear keeps us in our comfort zone and gladly takes the blame for our lack of progress. It can even be disguised as a voice of reason, preventing us from possible failures, heartache, and disappointments. How many times have you let fear turn you away from pursuing a goal, dream, or even a really great idea?

The day before the high ropes course challenge, I jotted down some ideas for this book. I've done this before. Actually, I've written down new ideas weekly and have even brainstormed many book titles and concepts.

The difference is that now I understand what prevented me from actually writing this book, finding out how to publish it, and from putting my story out in the world. I'm not going to use fear as the windshield to my future any longer. Fear can come along with me, as Elizabeth Gilbert writes,

"Fear.... You're allowed to have a seat and you're allowed to have a voice, but you are not allowed to have a vote. You're not allowed to touch the road maps... DUDE, you're not even allowed to touch the radio. But, above all else, my DEAR old familiar friend, you are absolutely FORBIDDEN to drive."

I uncovered all this and more from a high ropes course and some amazing coaches that supported me during that experience. Visiting a high ropes course has never been on my "to-do list" or even something that I thought, "Oh, that looks fun." I completed the course to be part of a team. To support my friends (many of whom I had just met days ago). To learn to trust others. To challenge myself. And, well, I didn't want to be left out.

I learned that people are awesome! Their coaching, encouragement and feedback helped me make it through. I learned that I can trust them to help guide me through something new. I learned it's important to pay attention to details, that I can ask for help, I can accept help, and I can face my fear and jump anyway.

If so many life-changing lessons can be gleaned from a ropes course, imagine what we can learn if we apply the same principles in our classrooms! I propose we create the right conditions for students to learn, not just the academic stuff but also the personal growth stuff (which may serve them better in the long run). The Buck Institute, the leader in Project-Based Learning, calls these "soft skills."

When students feel that people are awesome, that they can trust people to guide them through something new, that it's important to pay attention to detail, that they can ask for and receive help, and that when learning something new feels a little scary and they do it anyway, then learning opportunities multiply.

What if we could provide those conditions for our students? What would it take to consistently create the ultimate learning environment?

I've discovered some key factors that support optimal learning, help me make the biggest impact on my students, and keep me inspired and loving my job. If you notice an area where you shine already, you might choose to take it a step deeper. Become the guru in your district for that topic. Maybe even submit proposals to speak at local conferences and share your experiences with other teachers. If you, like many teachers, want to be perfect at ALL of the factors, start by picking one to make your own. Set a goal for how you want this to affect your students and teaching in the next 6 months. Revisit your goal and, like the rockstar I know you are, you'll be ready to implement the next area of focus when the time comes. After all, you're taking your precious time right now to devote to learning how to be a better teacher. That is the mark of an incredible teacher. I'm honored to be a part of your journey to revive your dream. ♡

Let's dig in!

Why Teach?

I have wanted to teach since I was 8 years old, mostly because I wanted to write on the chalkboard and use the red pen to grade papers. I'm fortunate enough to be living out that dream, though now that I'm 18 years in, chalkboards are nonexistent and grading papers is the last thing I want to do. Now I yearn for *more*. I have bigger dreams. I make vision boards. I want to make a difference in the world of education. I know I was put on this planet to teach. I want to help teachers stay passionate about their jobs without being pulled into the negativity that often accompanies the profession. I want school to be a source of inspiration for students, too.

After listening to an amazing interview with Marie Forleo and Dr. Tererai Trent, I realized that my visions showed ME reaching my goals - to become an author, to spend more time with my family, to pay off debt, to ride horses, to speak to educators, to reduce our carbon footprint. The dreams are mine, for ME and about ME, as if I am the center of the universe. After listening to Dr. Trent's humility, authenticity, passion, dedication, and wisdom, I realized my dreams are a part of the bigger picture, a global perspective. She said, "Your dreams in this life will have greater meaning when they are tied to the betterment of your community." Yes. This.

What are my dreams? Yes, to become a better person and a better teacher, and most importantly now, to support all the other dreamers who can "stand on my shoulders," as Dr. Trent says, and carry the dream onward. I am humbled. I am inspired. I am changed.

Why do I teach? I teach because I believe that all students deserve the opportunity to learn and be inspired, not just go to school.

"It's not about the education. It's not about the personal goals, neither is it about the personal financial goals, but it is about how our education and how our personal goals are connected to the greater good. That's what makes humanity, that's what makes who we are as people." -Dr. Trent

Why do you teach? If you don't like the first answer that comes to mind (*I do get the summers off...*) or the exhaustion as you think, "I used to love teaching... before I knew about all the testing, meetings, crazy parents, planning, grading, behavior issues, etc.," take some time to revisit your original dream to be a teacher. If you feel too far from that dream because you're so disenchanted with the education system, you're not alone. Heck, you may be in the majority. I know, because I was there too, and desperately trying to get out of teaching altogether.

LOVE LEADS TO LEARNING

Part 1

"Whoever loves much, performs much, and can accomplish much, and what is done in love is done well."
– Vincent Van Gogh

"If you don't first secure students' hearts, you don't have a shot at their brains."
– Angela Maiers

1

THE STORIES YOU BRING

My knees were visibly shaking as I wiped my sweaty hands on a napkin stuffed in my pocket and waited my turn.

2 minutes. 150 people.

I'd been charged with delivering an authentic, clear pitch to an audience of 150 people in less than two minutes. The backs of eight podcasting icons faced me on the stage behind me. Like the judges on *The Voice*, they turn around if they are moved by your message and feel you have something to offer their listeners.

I'm in a room full of entrepreneurs, not teachers. And I'm terrified. I had woken up at 4am to rehearse my pitch, and actually considered scrapping the whole thing.

What if I can't compose myself and I cry? I felt so much pressure, crying was definitely an option! What if I forget what to say? What if I freeze up and can't speak at all? What if I waste those two minutes and fail? I wasn't even worried if any of the icons would turn around at this point.

As I stood there rehearsing, it didn't feel right. I decided to rewrite my pitch, getting rid of the carefully scripted version that I had vetted and gotten approved by several coaches.

Then, ten minutes before the conference started, I practiced my newly crafted pitch alone in my hotel room. My story would take up the bulk of the two minutes I had to share, though I felt it was more important to share it.

In my original pitch, the following story was just one sentence, the longest sentence, but nonetheless, only one. The story was a catalyst for changing my relationship with teaching. I guess it makes sense to share that story with you here.

It was never in my realm of thinking that any 2nd grader would come to school wearing a white t-shirt with the word "killer" scribbled across the front with a black Sharpie.

Meet Michael. He was clean-cut, tall for his age, and seemed to be savvy beyond his years. The cuss words he knew and whispered to the other students were enough to make you cringe. The principal didn't share his file with me, or even give me a warning, because as I later learned, she wanted him to have a fresh start, without any labels or judgments.

I never dreamt that I'd have students throwing chairs, carving cuss words in the bathroom stall, and causing extreme anxiety for other students, as they did their best to avoid being hit by fists and flying objects. I didn't sign up for this. No one would sign up for this.

Little did I know, this 8-year-old boy would make me rethink my career in teaching, and ultimately change the trajectory of my entire career.

This was 2013, in the middle of my twelfth year of teaching, which was no longer my dream. It was my burden. I resented the time I spent grading and planning because it took away from time with my family. My career consisted of venting in the copy room, complaining about how bad the students were in the lunchroom, wishing there was a downed electric pole so that school would be canceled, and browsing local job ads so that I could quit.

Those negative thoughts had been building for five years and teaching Michael was the tipping point.

Michael's daily agenda included throwing things during read aloud, refusing to work during writer's workshop, tripping students when they walked by his desk, and playing sniper at recess. Seriously, he'd put his black hood over his head and run around pretending to shoot kids. My assistant principal showed me footage from recess that he had gotten from our security cameras. The visual was disturbing, to say the least. Little kids were running away in frantic groups as a hooded figure hunted them down. You couldn't tell he wasn't holding a real gun. Not a kid likely to get awarded "Student of the Week."

It was really hard to like this kid.

Learning how to deal with Michael's behavior, teach the rest of the class, and not go home hating my job was a challenge. I felt offended, defeated, angry, and resentful (towards Michael, his parents, and even the administrators). Beautiful teaching resume, right? Up for grabs! One resentful, angry 2nd grade teacher ready to be offended by your child's behavior. Hire her today! Eek.

And finally, my breaking point. That pivotal day when Michael proudly came to school wearing that white t-shirt, announcing, "KILLER."

I remember being disgusted. Horrified. I thought, "This is why I need to get out of teaching. I can't send my son to this school."

After complaining to my husband, other teachers, and using Michael and his idea of a cool shirt as more leverage to build my case to quit teaching, I noticed a subtle twinge. A twinge that led me to realize I had become exactly who I never wanted to become. I was that negative, pessimistic teacher, despising her job.

With the enormity of that realization, I decided to get curious and investigate what this twinge was all about. I let myself feel it a bit more and found that the twinge was encouraging a hint of compassion. And it was coming from my heart. Now the anger was replaced with something kinder and I decided to actually listen to it.

Michael needs me. He needs someone to love him. How can I support him? What if I didn't take his behavior personally - if I could stop being the victim, stop making it all about me? *My* day was ruined. *My* teaching was interrupted. *My* plan time was consumed by emails about Michael.

What if I could respond from my heart, instead of from my own ego and fear?

This was different.

Different sounded better. I needed different, because my current batch of emotions was driving me to quit the education profession altogether.

I set the intention to let go of my ego - you know, the one that wants the perfect class, all students to love me, and wants to teach, what I signed up to do when I got a teaching degree. Instead, I accepted the fact that Michael wasn't going to behave like his peers. I remembered a quote by Jane Nelson, "A misbehaving child is a discouraged child." Well, Michael must be REALLY discouraged.

What does a discouraged child need? Patience, love, kindness, compassion, acceptance, consistency, stability, rapport, grace. Not resentment, anger, frustration, fear, power struggles, or condemnation...

This turn around would require authenticity - I couldn't fake compassion and acceptance. I'd need to learn how to love Michael.

Instead of me "teaching him a lesson," I was going to learn the lesson.

I thought that perhaps the most powerful teaching can be done from this different place, a heart space. When I teach from that place, maybe Michael's mind could be opened to a new relationship that would also lead to learning. The bulk of teaching is heavy on the academics, that's the whole point of our education system—kids need to read, write and do arithmetic. This new type of teaching would involve a shift in my operating system and my ego. I needed to choose a different perspective and constantly reflect on my actions.

It wasn't easy. I had to face those feelings of resentment, fear, anger, and even disgust when Michael would misbehave. I tried to not take offense. I checked in on him more often, not to "catch" him, but to truly see how he was doing. I did my best to let him know that I cared, I forgave him, and that I saw him as an 8 year old boy needing some positive attention.

Sometimes I doubted if this was really working, because I still got frustrated when he would walk by and hit another child in the back of the head, just when I turned to help another student. I still got angry when he would deny his behavior when everyone clearly knew he did it.

One rough day, my teaching partner was out so our class had a sub in the morning. I came in around lunch time to find my students running up to me in the hallway.

"Mrs. Molitor! Michael yelled at the teacher and threw things!" they told me. Students were yelling out, "He wouldn't listen to the teacher! She chased him around the room. He said bad words. I was worried!"

My class had been evacuated from our classroom because Michael was out of control. And now they couldn't find him!

I walked into our classroom and called his name. I heard sniffling and found him hiding, curled up on the bottom of a bookshelf.

It never occurred to me that Michael had the capacity to cry. He always showed such a tough, even violent, exterior. And now here he was, a real 8 year old boy, vulnerable, feeling broken, and in need of some grace.

"It's ok. Come on out," I said softly as I knelt on the carpet and giving him space. Slowly he crawled out to me, sobbing, and buried his head.

I was shocked. Part of me was so angry at him. The other part of me, the part that remembered to tap into the heart space, realized that he felt scared and unsure. And the crazy exciting thing is he willingly and vulnerably came to me when he was in trouble. Somehow I must have earned his trust.

We walked out to the hallway and he still clung to me, crying. Two administrators sped down the hallway toward us. Typically, I'd be relieved and eager to hear them reprimand Michael. I'd feel supported and validated as if they would say, "Yes, your job is tough and Michael is very challenging to work with. We'll take care of it from here. He won't be causing you any more problems."

But that's not how I felt.

I wanted more time with Michael. I wanted him to know that he was safe. I wanted to hear about what had transpired, from his perspective. I wanted him to know that I cared about him. That he mattered. That his choices don't define him.

I wanted to defend him and lessen the consequences. I wanted the administrators to go easy on him, to understand that he's hurting, feeling broken, and needing more support than being suspended.

I realized that this kid needed me. Not to teach him the standards and keep him in line. He needed someone to see him, not his behaviors. To connect with him.

An awareness settled into my bones.

Start with the heart.

Truly connecting with students on a heart level is the powerful beginning of good, meaningful, life-changing teaching. This connection takes rapport to a different level - beyond smiles and high fives.

So through my story, I landed on my message:

Start with the heart, and as if by magic, the mind also opens to learning.

By investigating another perspective and making the choice to offer grace more often than resentment, I had come so far. Thanks to Michael, I'd stretched myself, found my why, and was ready to love more kids.

By the time I got to the end of my speech, I was barely getting the words out and fighting back tears. My teaching journey had served me well.

I don't remember how many icons turned around. It didn't matter. I had found a new light to guide me. I discovered a path that encouraged resiliency. Instead of getting beaten down, feeling like "they" keep adding to my plate, like the expectations get higher and the supports get taken away, I felt hopeful and empowered. I am only one, though if I could support other teachers in embracing resiliency, we could change the world. Let's take those crumpled up pieces of paper that life throws our way and repurpose them so that we shine with passion and love.

What's your story? Why do you stay in teaching?

In times of doubt or stress, remember - we've all got the stories that make us want to quit. But I challenge you to go into that heart place, and find the stories that make you want to stay.

2

THE MYTHS OF RAPPORT

Myth #1: Good rapport is primarily established based on comprehensive knowledge of a student; his strengths, his friends, his food allergies, his parents' work schedules, his reading level, his favorite shoes...

One definition of rapport is "a close and harmonious relationship in which the people understand each other's feelings or ideas and communicate well."

Good rapport starts with smiling and greeting students by the door. But it's also more than that. It goes beyond knowing which sports they play and if they live with both parents. Rapport goes deeper. Rapport takes time, trust, and commitment to develop. The more I grasp what rapport truly means, the more I realize that building rapport can be tricky, even when you're family! True rapport starts with genuine interest in students - *especially* when they misbehave. It involves more grace than you think you have. Ultimately, it requires an awareness and a letting go of the ego during those moments when we get offended because Tommy threw a pencil while you were teaching and then refused to sit in his chair to work on his assignment. I don't know about you, but my first reaction would be to offer consequences: write him up, threaten to call his mom, and encourage a power struggle. However, rapport doesn't encourage battles, especially when it involves a child. Rapport cares enough to find out why Tommy is struggling to participate. Rapport means checking in with the ego. "Why am I so mad? Should I calm down before acting? Is my response actually retaliation?"

I was helping out in a 1st grade music class, and all the students were sitting on their carpet squares on the floor. One student was wiggling around and must have been chatting with a neighbor. The teacher said, "AJ, move your carpet square here," as she pointed to the far side of the room, which happened to be close to me. The disappointment and frustration showed in his eyes and slumped shoulders. As he dropped to the floor, I looked over at him and smiled. I whispered, "It's ok."

We went through the rest of class and I made sure to give him a few extra smiles. At the end of class, he asked if I could play with him at recess. Oh my goodness!! I had connected with this kiddo so quickly and must have given him the idea that I saw him and he mattered. His little mishap on the carpet didn't define him.

Two days later I happened to be in his homeroom class and he waved at me. It took me a few minutes to remember who he was. He asked if I could help him with his writing. "Sure!" I told him as I knelt beside his desk. I helped him spell a few words and kept him focused on the task. His face was taut as he worked hard to hold the pencil and form his letters. He told me, "I never finish my sentences, but with your help, I just might do it!" He really didn't need much support, he just needed to know it was there. I reinforced his nice handwriting and his hard work. I walked away to help another student, and he waved me back after a few minutes. I checked in again, and he told me that was the most he ever wrote about the scientist of the day. As I walked out the door, he again asked me to play with him at recess and if I could come back the following day. He pulled on my heartstrings quite a bit!!

AJ had a wonderful teacher who loved him dearly. I have a feeling he had been reprimanded often by other teachers, and he most likely had had behavior issues since he started school. I imagine teaching this kid had been tricky. He didn't sit properly. He didn't pay attention. He didn't raise his hand. He was impulsive and could be physical with other students. He was demanding and wouldn't problem solve simple problems. These behaviors don't match our classroom expectations. They can be frustrating. However, there needs to be different expectations for students like AJ.

Our time is limited, and we simply have too many standards to fit in one school year. I get it. That was one of the many stressors I let burn me out. However, I found that if we teach from our heart space more often, students are more receptive to learning. This deeper rapport seems to help students learn more in the time we have. Those invisible barriers and questions like: "Does she like me?" "Does she think I'm a brat?" "Why do I keep getting in trouble?" "When can I go home?" disappear from the mindspace and make room for academics.

Myth #2: You can fake rapport.

Kids know. Just like dogs seem to know who they can trust right away, kids know if you're friendly or trustworthy, if you're authentic or just going through the motions, if you believe in them or you doubt they'll have any success later in life.

If you ask any teacher, most will say they believe all students can learn and they believe in their students. However, I've also been in the lunchroom, work room, and in the hallways after school. I've heard how teachers talk about kids when they aren't in the room and, holy moly, I sure hope none of the students ever catch wind of those conversations.

Teaching is hard. I love how Michael Bonner says that students are human first. The key to building rapport is cultivating authentic relationships - relationships that don't change when we close the door.

Venting is common across all professions. We might listen to our friends vent about the day they've had or complain about the horrible service at the local restaurant. When we spend our time rehashing the bad experiences of our day, we spend even more time dwelling in negativity. This is a human thing, not a teacher thing. Alison Ledgerwood, a social psychologist at UC Davis spoke to this in a TED Talk. She says we're wired to seek out negativity and even "hold onto it." She explains, "Our view of the world tends to tilt towards the negative... we have to work harder to see the upside of things." *Getting stuck in the negatives (and how to get unstuck)* | Alison Ledgerwood | TEDxUCDavis

The silver lining is that we can choose to seek out positivity. When we stop talking about all the ick and focus on the great things happening in our lives, great things seem to happen more. Positive people attract positive people. This spills over in the classroom, too.

Don't get me wrong. There are definitely bad days. However, we can choose to dwell on all those terrible things and vent often, or we can problem solve and search for solutions.

If you want better rapport with your students, monitor how you talk about them when they're not in the room. Notice how you talk about Susie's mom who emails you 13 times a day, or Johnny's grandma who forgot to give him his meds this morning, or Sarah's mom who walks her to her 5th grade classroom every morning.

First notice. Then choose: to vent, or let go and seek solutions. Authenticity isn't just speaking politely when there's a parent helper nearby. Authenticity is shown through your actions during the good times *and* the bad. It's easy to be positive and cheery when things are going well. It's not as easy when we get a flat tire on the way to work, drop our coffee in the parking lot, and then find out we missed a meeting.

Optimism is a choice that we can make a habit.

If we're having a bad day, it'd be a great teachable moment to share with students about how to navigate the downs. They get to see you as human too, making mistakes, and rising above. It's also a powerful lesson that can rewire our brain to shift towards the positive.

Myth #3: Kids know they matter.

You know those viral videos that people share on Facebook? Yes, the cat and cucumber videos are hilarious, but I'm talking about something a bit more inspiring. I came across a video that highlighted a school's use of a powerful phrase for students to finish: I wish my teacher knew....

I was blown away by the insight and vulnerability embedded in each student response. So much so that I decided to try it out with a group of my students.

First thing on a September morning, I asked a group of about twenty 5th graders to finish the phrase, "I wish my teacher knew..." on a post-it.

Building rapport has always been a strength for me. I seem to connect really well with kids, and people in general. But after seeing my students' responses, I decided I could still improve in this area.

The students had placed the post-its on my desk and had gotten to work on their next task. I picked up a few post-its... and couldn't stop reading them. I was touched, surprised, and even baffled as I read.

- I wish my teacher knew my brother is autistic.
- I wish my teacher knew that 2 of my cats ran away and 2 of them drowned in my pool and I can't get over it.
- I wish my teacher knew that I don't always get along with partners, and friends...
- I wish my teacher knew that I love to go outside and be by myself.
- I wish my teacher knew that my granny died and I'm still really sad.
- I wish my teacher knew that I can't really help moving a lot and fidget.

After reading a few, I interrupted the students. I felt there was this heart space that had opened and I wanted to acknowledge it, and I had a follow-up question. I thanked my students for sharing so vulnerably and authentically, and asked, "You shared such deeply personal wishes. Why is it important to you that your teacher knows these things about you?"

Again, the beautiful insight from my 5th graders wowed me.

"My teacher will understand me more."

"My teacher will make connections to me."

"I'll know I matter."

"I'll know my teacher cares."

Read those again and let those responses sit with you. Of course I want my students to know they matter! Don't they see that they matter when I greet them at the door, smile at them, check-in with them, help with friendship arguments, and even give them money to buy lunch?

Maybe not. Maybe that's not enough to really tap into their heart.

As a mom, I know how hectic the morning routine can be. After some reflection, I discovered that some mornings I don't even give my own kids eye contact. I'm making breakfast, asking them to get dressed (for the third time), making a grocery list, fixing my hair, feeding the dogs and packing lunches (trying hard not to mix-up the last two). We hurry along every morning. I give them hugs, though they're quick and almost feel routine. I wondered if my kids knew they mattered.

Dr. Shefali, a parenting expert and author, says children want to know three things:

1. Do I matter?
2. Am I worthy?
3. Am I seen?

I decided I would be more purposeful with my morning routine and offering my own kids the opportunity to know I really see them. Now I make it a point to look them in the eyes, smile, tell them I love them, and take those few seconds to let them feel it, not just go through the gestures.

My teaching life is quite similar. Make copies, send emails, pray there's only one voicemail message while the persistent little red message light hints otherwise, check in with my team to revise our math plans due to the assembly we forgot about, go to a staff meeting where I learn the fire drill is during my plan time (again?!), and then realize I don't have even 20 seconds to pee before the kids arrive.

Eye contact. Not up there on the priority list.

I remembered the kids responses. "I'll know I matter." And I decided to stretch myself.

Eye contact moved up the priority list. Along with it, I implemented a beginning of the day warm-up that I called an opener (more on that in Chapter 3).

You'd think that looking at students more often is easy peasy. Yes, looking at them is simple, but eye contact is different. This requires more attention and focus on the student and detracts from multitasking. Teaching seems to require multitasking. Somehow I can check email, staple papers, and answer questions from students at the same time. Does this show the students they matter? What if you showed up to a meeting with your superintendent, and she was standing in her office shuffling through papers while she was on hold with the Department of Education. Would you feel important? I'd feel rushed and a bit nervous as I tried to map out what I would say so that I didn't waste her time.

Eye contact says, "I see you. I hear you. You matter. You are worthy of my time." Eye contact might interfere with checking email, grading, and stapling papers, but the payoff will be worth it.

I'm still guilty. My to-do list feels longer than Santa's naughty list. I hit the ground running and never feel caught up. I remember daydreaming about getting an office job where I could sit in my own space, all day long, and not have to answer a million questions, plan 6 different lessons, pick up trash at the end of the day, and have to monitor anyone during my lunch... oh, and I could go OUT to lunch!

I still need to remind myself to slow down, breathe, and let students know they're worthy of my time. After all, I teach children, not papers or emails. I teach children.

3

THE MOST POWERFUL QUESTIONS

Ask the right questions, and the answers will always reveal themselves.
-Oprah Winfrey

What are your most incredible teaching accomplishments?

For me, one is staying in education. I trusted my gut that teaching is where I should be. I'm working hard to avoid complaining and venting about all the problems in our schools and I've started using my energies towards finding solutions. Even teeny solutions, like finding a solid writing curriculum for our new 4th grade ELA teacher or covering for a teacher so she could attend a meeting, are steps in the right direction. It just doesn't make sense to complain about our lack of resources or why the administration didn't get a sub for a teacher to attend a crucial meeting about a student.

Thinking about your most incredible teaching accomplishments gets you thinking about positives - things you're proud of, the highlights of your career. As educators we also get to direct a student's line of thinking. We can frame questions to set the stage for positivity, optimism, and growth... or for negativity, shame, and guilt. In an article in the

Harvard Business Review, *The Questions Good Coaches Ask,* Amy Jen Su writes,

> The right question can stop her in her tracks as she finally sees her own actions from a different perspective or envisions a new solution to an old problem. The most important thing to keep in mind while composing (and delivering) coaching questions is that you need to be genuinely curious about the answers.

What about this question: What traits are commendable in bullies?

When I first thought about my response to that question I thought, "Hmph, nothing. What could be commendable about a bully? That's a stupid question."

Here's the thing - If you really consider the question, there are some things about bullies that we could find favorable. They're persistent, committed, outgoing, deliberate, brave, risk-takers, etc. The context of the question veers away from the negative connotation of bullies and gives us a different perspective.

Now consider this one: What's the best thing teaching has done for your life?

This question assumes that teaching IS making a positive impact in your life. We can use a similar question in our problem-solving meetings about students. *What's the biggest contribution Joey has made to your classroom? How is he helping you grow as a teacher?*

"Asking the right questions is as important as answering them," says Benoit Mendelbrot. For example, "Why do you keep getting in trouble?" and "What's wrong with you?" are both lousy questions. Neither feel good or empower the student. On the other hand, asking "How can I help you turn this around?" and "Why is recess important to you?" will encourage a thoughtful, honest answer. Understanding the power of our questions is helpful for both teachers and parents as we upgrade our discussions with children. Consider Madeleine L'Engle's suggestion, "I wish that we worried more about asking the right questions instead of being so hung up on finding the answers."

Top Tips for Asking Thoughtful Questions

1. Give the student the benefit of the doubt.
2. Ask from a place of curiosity, not anger, blame, or shame.
3. Soften so the student can answer honestly.
4. Consider how you can promote a learning opportunity, versus a "gotcha."
5. Listen. Really listen.

Heart-Based Questions

I started collecting valuable questions and created what I call an opener or warm-up for students (though I also use them with teachers). Starting the day with these questions has been insightful in helping me know and understand my students better. You can find the full opener in the resource section at the end of this book. It might be helpful to share these questions with your team, so that you can all support each other through the sticky moments when complaining hijacks your meeting.

What are you bringing with you today?

I'm not looking for a literal response such as my backpack, pencil, etc. I'm looking for the invisible stuff kids carry: worry about their cat, concern for their grandmother, excitement about a birthday party, frustration about something that happened on the bus. This question helps me know who to check in with a bit more, who isn't emotionally ready to learn how to multiply decimals or compare fractions, and who may be misbehaving due to circumstances beyond their control.

What are you ready to let go of today, or what have you been struggling with?

A 5th grader was ready to let go of arguing with her mom, another was ready to let go of being late for school, and another was ready to let go of having trouble sleeping. This question also opens up a whole new level of rapport. Not only do I learn more about students, but students make bigger connections to each other. One 1st grade teacher started using the opener questions and noticed more of her students playing together at recess. Their groups were much larger and students seemed to relate more to one another.

What has gone well for you this week?

What is one thing you can do today that you'll be proud of?

Sit for a few moments & visualize how you'd like today to go. Get specific with how you want to feel, act, and achieve.

These prompts all direct students towards positive scenarios, reflecting on something that's already gone well (good trend) & more ideas to empower them to keep that trend going.

Secret Recipe for Student Success

❤ + ? = learning

Armed with these new, fun, and inexpensive strategies, I began giving students more eye contact, started slowing down my multi-tasking, and started asking students different questions.

My rapport with kids skyrocketed! As I made stronger connections with my students, I was able to share these powerful tips with parents. I stopped cringing when I saw the red message light blinking on my phone.

I knew more about my students on a much larger scale - not just academics. I got to know my students as people and teaching people was more rewarding than teaching curriculum. I was again reminded that powerful teaching is done through the heart. When we start there, as if by magic, the mind also opens to learning.

Which brings me to the research. Have you heard about HeartMath? It's a concept I had never been taught in schools, universities, or in any professional development that I've ever attended. Here's a quick summary:

Most of us have been taught in school that the heart is constantly responding to "orders" sent by the brain in the form of neural signals. However, it is not as commonly known that the heart actually sends more signals to the brain than the brain sends to the heart! Moreover, these heart signals have a significant effect on brain function – influencing emotional processing as well as higher cognitive faculties such as attention, perception, memory, and problem-solving. In other words, not only does the heart respond to the brain, but the brain continuously responds to the heart. https://www.heartmath.com/science/ or visit heartmath.org

So, there is evidence that the heart is a great place to start as we continue this journey to support our students' learning.

I invested in the Inner Balance Trainer from HeartMath and already have some ideas for using their app with students as we incorporate more mindfulness into our classrooms.

Teachers have known about building rapport for years, but I think we've underestimated the power it can have on learning when we make truly authentic, loving connections with our students.

CULTIVATING THINKERS

Part 2

"We are not taught to be thinkers, but reflectors of our culture. Let's teach our children to be thinkers."
– Jacque Fesco

"Education is not the learning of facts, but the training of the mind to think."
– Albert Einstein

4

STUDENT ENGAGEMENT SECRETS

My husband comes home and notices my computer on the counter, as a robot-like voice echoes throughout the kitchen. I'm cooking dinner, overseeing the kids' homework, feeding the dogs, and "watching" the latest safety training module required by the state. Please don't tell on me! I do *listen* to the information... as I'm stirring the veggies, checking spelling, scooping dog food, and kissing my hubby hello.

It's just so hard to listen to that impersonal voice talk about things I either already know or only need to memorize long enough to pass a quiz. Seriously, do I really need to know *all* the different types and classes of fires and the chemicals used to put them out? I teach 3rd grade. Sadly, in this day and age, we should probably be learning about the different types of guns and how they range in destructiveness. Historically it seems there are far more incidents of gun violence at school than fires.

My point is that I'm not going to pay attention if the instruction seems insincere, irrelevant, and delivered by a robot. Kids aren't either. The tricky part is, most of the teaching aids we're given are just as boring, irrelevant, or plainly out-dated.

So how can we truly engage students so that:

1. everyone participates
2. learning is fun
3. they still like us at the end of the day, and
4. they run home excitedly jabbering about the awesome lesson we delivered today?

Easy peasy, right?

Planning spectacular, exemplary lessons can consume your days, evenings and weekends. That's why Teachers Pay Teachers continues to be so successful. Instead of spending my time creating fun, hands-on activities, it'd be so much easier to pay a few bucks for a worksheet with cutie pics and borders that already seems engaging. I have pretty specific criteria for activities and worksheets, though, and the cute font and pics aren't top on my list.

Consider the elements included in the powerful *R.A.C.E. Checklist* when you plan or vet an activity.

Let's break it down a bit.

Implementing R.A.C.E.

R.elevancy

How many times have you sat through a meeting, training or class and wondered, "Why are we learning this?" Our adult brain can reason, "If I finish this class, I'll be one class closer to achieving my masters degree," or "When I finish this training, I'll be certified to administer the state test." We can chock up all the uselessness to something we just gotta do. Even that can be a tough pill to swallow sometimes. However, a child may not care that she'll pass her test, get an A, or be able to divide bigger numbers.

While realizing we need to complete something just to do the next thing may be useful to understand and experience, we don't want students to wonder daily why school is important. Shoot, our days contain enough mandated "check-box" activities already: fundraiser assemblies, unnecessary meetings, interim reports, common assessments, state testing, etc.

Even fire and tornado drills can become one of those things we do to check off a box. Sometimes I worry that since we schedule the drills, making sure to avoid lunch and transition times, that we won't know what the heck to do in a real emergency! We teach children to "Be quiet, line up, and follow me out of the building. Remember, the last one out should close the door!" And just like that, we're outside waiting patiently to be let back inside.

We all want to know if something is worth learning. Telling students, "It will be on the test," or "You'll need this when you're in college," only works on the select students who care about grades and think that getting good scores equals success. For the rest, we've got to be more transparent. Why are we learning this? Even if it's just a hoop to jump through, how can we teach it in a relevant way? After all, we want to develop *thinkers,* not *memorizers.*

If students are questioning the relevancy of your lesson, they've probably already checked out.

Chandler Bolt, the entrepreneur who started the highly successful Self-Publishing School (you're reading a bit of that proof right now!), dropped out of college after a few years in. He wanted to learn how to start, grow, and maintain a business. When he started college, he anticipated studying the ins and outs of running a business... only to discover that he had to take all these core classes as part of the graduation requirement for any major. He decided to stick it out until he could take business courses. Here's how he explains it in his book, Published.

To make matters worse, after finally attending a few business classes, I realized I was learning how to run a business from professors who had never run businesses before... and that didn't make much sense to me.

I learn by doing, not by theory. Maybe you're the same way.

In the middle of a lesson I'd ask, "This is really awesome! I'm curious about how you're using this in your business?" The most frequent response was, "Well,

I actually don't have a business. I learned this from a textbook during my MBA."

Sigh... While I was going back and forth between internships and class, I quickly found myself paying less and less attention to the lectures. ***The "traditional class setting" rapidly began to mean nothing to me.*** *After I completed an internship, I realized my personal goal was to learn, not earn a degree. I thought to myself, "Why are you wasting your time sitting through lectures when you could actually be out in the real world, running a real business? That's the way to learn!" (p. 12)*

Now, Chandler is helping people all over the world publish books on their own. He figured out how to publish a book and run a business from his own experiences - not from a degree in literature or business.

Our traditional schooling model seems to provide lots of hoops for students to jump through simply in order to get to the next set of hoops. The end game, a high school diploma, sets students up for even more hoops once they get to college. However, If students pursue a vocational school, they begin learning the trade right away. They become immersed in their work of cutting hair, giving massages, welding, or fixing cars. This 'learning by doing' happens after 13 years of traditional schooling, and by then, we've already missed the boat with so many students. School seems to be failing those who really want to learn.

We've got to find a way to stop playing hoops. What do students *want* to learn? I recently met a social studies teacher from Sycamore High School in Cincinnati, Ohio, who asks this question on a daily basis. He was bold enough to take a risk and learn the answer. He gave his students the list of standards they were supposed to master in a specific social studies class and told them, "Here's what you need to know, decide how you'll learn it." Crazy, right?! He eagerly shared about the projects students decided to pursue. One student wasn't really interested in history. He wanted to learn more about economics, so he combined the two in a study on the costs of war.

Chatting with this teacher, who humbly explains that this process isn't perfect, started a fire in me! On my way home, I called my boss, the

Director of Learning and Innovation. I told him, "Let's do this for our students. Let's shake up education!" He laughed at my excitement and agreed with my rationale. It sounded too easy, too simple, and yet too big to even know where to start.

Kids deserve to learn - not memorize so they can regurgitate facts and steps on a test. Incorporating experiences that are **relevant to them** will take us in the right direction.

A.TTENTION GRABBER

Remember how I started the introduction to this book? (If you skipped it, that's ok, I tend to skip intros to jump into the content too. Though how about you revisit it. Just read the first few lines and come back. Don't worry, I'll wait for you.)

Were you able to just read the first paragraph? I'm curious! I hope the intro was engaging enough to convince you to read the whole thing.

Telling stories is my superpower. I love sharing a personal story with kids or teachers and knowing I've got their attention. Piquing student interest from the get-go is so important! This is also known as the "hook." Hooks in the classroom can be telling a story, listening to a song, watching a video clip, reading a picture book or a snippet from a chapter book, sharing an unsolved mystery, using an object or manipulatives, or explaining a real-life problem you have.

In my first few years of teaching, I had fabulous colleagues (shout out to Katie Droder and Liz Messerschmitt) to plan with. We created the ultimate mystery unit for October that included two differentiated choice boards for two different novels: Cam Jansen and the Stolen Diamonds and The Boxcar Children and The Pizza Mystery. Each choice board focused on the same elements (character traits, elements of a mystery, and vocabulary), though at varying degrees of difficulty. To introduce this unit, we created a riddle poem as clues and hid them throughout the school. Here's how it started:

. . .

Clue #1:

(Clue #1 was in our lunch card drawer by the office.)

This is where the cards should be,

Sorry, check the attendance tree.

Clue #2:

(Clue #2 was on our classroom attendance chart.)

I clean and sweep for you each day,

Where do you go indoors to play?

Clue #3:

(Clue #3 was in our indoor recess cabinet.)

Your room was left such a mess,

Where can I let out all my stress?

(Clue #4 was in our worry jar.)

Each clue gave us an idea about where to look for the next clue. When students first entered the classroom, there were chairs out of place, pawprints and shoe prints on the floor, the window was open just a bit (footprints led to the window), and when our students went to get their lunch cards, they were missing. You better believe the students were so excited! I pretended to have this big lesson to get through, though noticing their excitement as they started collecting clues, I told them we better solve this mystery so that we could find our lunch cards.

We brainstormed what each clue could mean and that since they were numbered, there must be more. The clues ended with us bringing something sweet to our custodian, who had to come back to school to finish cleaning up our messy room. He lives close and brought his dog along with him and snuck in our open window because he forgot his keys. He wanted to teach us a lesson about leaving the room so messy.

Students were eager to read mysteries after they had so much detective experience already and they made sure to pick up the floor better at the end of the day too.

After reading The Wild Card by Hope and Wade King last summer, our elementary set a goal for each grade level team to do two room transformations. We had all sorts of creative endeavors: café, rainforest, a basketball championship, settings from Dr. Suess's stories, and a boot camp complete with camouflage and military boots. By changing the students' surroundings, we were able to revitalize their interest in the upcoming lessons.

What creative ways can you grab your students' attention? Here are a few of my favorites:

- Humor
- Stories/ Drama
- Vulnerability
- Authenticity
- Mystery/ Suspense
- Music
- Movement
- Puzzler/ Challenge
- Curiosity hook- Curiosity not only increases motivation to learn, but it also produces chemical changes in the brain that improve memory. Gruber, M. J., Gelman, B. D., & Ranganath, C. (2014) States of Curiosity Modulate Hippocampus-Dependent Learning via the Dopaminergic Circuit. *Neuron*, *84*(2), 486-496. https://doi.org/10.1016/j.neuron.2014.08.060

C.hallenge

I thought about using the word "differentiation" though I feel it's easier to simplify an assignment than it is to extend it. So while the goal is to differentiate, the truth is, teachers often struggle more to teach those students who either already know the content we're about to introduce, or they pick it up in 5 minutes and finish before you're even done giving directions.

I also find that challenges are easier to come up with when you're thinking about relevant tasks and you're posing the challenge as a question. Instead of telling students to solve 5 word problems or read Chapter 4 of their novel, let's take the task and turn it into an open-ended, relevant, higher-level question.

If the goal is to add 2-digit numbers (like 28 + 93), what could the students do to really go beyond the numbers and be challenged? Not necessarily more of the same or even a bigger problem (288 + 933). That would be like listening to my robot modules for 45 minutes instead of 35 minutes or "getting" to do the robot's advanced level combustible training program. No thank you!

How is knowing how and being able to add 2-digit numbers going to benefit your students? Think about something you're genuinely curious about or better yet, what are the students curious about? Or consider events that are happening in your school, like carnivals, book fairs, spirit week, etc. If you get really specific, the relevancy of your task may not be as relevant to another teacher in the same grade - and that's ok!!

You might pose any of the following questions:

- If you brought $3 to buy lunch in our cafeteria, what are all the possible ways to spend it? What is the healthiest option?
- Our school gets 10 cents for every dollar spent on books at the book fair. How much would we need to sell in order to earn $195? What if our goal was to earn $12,000?
- What patterns do you notice when you add numbers in the twenties to numbers in the eighties?
- What are all the possible numbers you can make when you

add numbers with at least 2 tens to numbers with at least 8 tens? Why is figuring this out important?
- How could we show how much profit our school made from the last book fair?
- How would adding 28 + 93 be similar to adding 3,428 + 8,793?

In reading, you might ask the following:

- As you read Chapter 4, find and record evidence of the main character's growth mindset. What are her strengths and what areas should she work on? What do you predict she'll be doing in 10 years? Why?
- Imagine the main character was preparing to ride on a plane or bus for the first time. Based on what you know about the character, what would she pack and what would her bags look like? Where would she be going and why?
- Write a summary of the book in 20 words or less. Then, figure out how to make the most of your words and choose the top 3 words as your 3-word summary.
- Choose a character and switch one of the following: gender, race, or age (reverse the digits). How would the story line change? How would the other characters respond?

Keeping students thinking is a biggie! Simply asking questions isn't going to cut it. We've got to stretch ourselves. Can you connect a concept to a movie, a famous actor, a song, or a fad? Furthermore, can you link that connection to an open-ended question? I'll share some examples below. I purposefully did not add grade levels. Can you tweak the questions to make them more fitting for your students? You might change the movie title, simplify the question, or ramp up the expectations. The question might be suitable for your entire class, or just the thing needed to challenge one student.

What Might Interest Kids	Rich, Open-Ended Questions
The Secret Life of Pets movie	• (Science) Which animal relationships in *The Secret Life of Pets* movie are the least likely to happen in real life? Why is that? Which relationships are the most likely to happen? • (ELA) Choose 2 characters from *The Secret Life of Pets* movie and create a "Wanted" poster for each one. Be sure to use as many descriptive character traits as you can and explain with great detail what it is that each character did to be "wanted." Then determine which character should have the greater reward.

Video Games	• (ELA) Choose a video game that you played recently and write a powerful, 5-sentence summary of the highlights of the game. Keep in mind that I may not have played this game so be careful and specific in your summary. You might consider what your goal was, what obstacles were in your way, and how the game ended. I'd be interested to know what you learned from that specific session. • (Science) What inaccuracies or misconceptions about geology can be found in minecraft? Write a guidebook for young minecraft players, explaining the truth about different rocks and minerals. You might discuss the durability of each material and/ or the scientific categories that each material fits in. • (Social Studies) Create a timeline showing the history of 2 of your favorite video games. Your timeline should include 8 significant events, showing how the video game came to be what it is today.

Sports	• (ELA) Write a letter to one of your favorite sports players explaining which main character he/ she would be most suited to play in a movie. Give 3 specific examples and add some persuasive language as you convince the player to consider trying out for the new role. • (Math) In sports, we often aim for a certain number or average when we compete- we're always trying to win or show improvement. When I rode dressage, a 65% was a decent score. Think about a sport you play. What 5-10 scores would make a decent average (or better) by the end of the season? Break down the scores for us. What do they mean? What would it take for you to actually achieve that average? Create a product to highlight your scores, the breakdown of each one, and the work it would take to achieve those scores. • (Math) Sort all the different sports you can think of into 3 categories. Which category has the most sports? Why do you think that is? Create a chart or graph showing the different categories and how each sport fits into a specific category. Also create a new sport, explain which category it fits into, and share the math we might use during the game.

E.motion

Now to put the icing on the cake! We've got to evoke some emotion. Why, you ask?

Because I know I feel more connected to a presenter when she tells me her best friend was just diagnosed with breast cancer and it's changing her life too. Or when she tells a hilarious story about her fake tooth falling out as she goes into labor and she was so worried about keeping her mouth shut (it was a prominent tooth) that it distracted her from labor pains! These stories help us connect because we see the presenter, who has similar ups and downs, is human too. And if you can't think of a good story to tell, feel free to make up a tall tale. I'm pretty sure my acting skills have developed nicely over the years.

Here's a true story I shared with my 5th graders to introduce a fraction lesson.

Edwin (remember that cutie who is so helpful in resolving clogged toilets?) asked me if I would take his iPhone with us to the pumpkin farm so he could take pictures. I told him no because I'll have my phone. So he left it on the coffee table.

When we got home, he couldn't find his phone. I assured him that it would turn up. He got upset and told me Cecelia (who was only 5) took it. He had no evidence that she took it, he only said, "I just know she did it."

So, trying to disguise my skepticism, I asked Cecelia, "Honey, did you take Edwin's phone?"

"No, Mama," came the sweet reply.

Edwin was adamant that Cecelia took it, so he went in her room to look for it. That didn't go over well with Cecelia, so I intervened and told him to leave her alone. It would turn up.

At bedtime that evening, we still didn't have the phone. I told him for sure we'd find it the following day.

I picked the kids up from school the next day, and Edwin was still grumpy about his phone. Cecelia was chattering happily from the back seat and nonchalantly said, "Wouldn't it be funny if Edwin's phone teleported and ended up under my pillow?"

Edwin immediately yelled, "It better not!!! You took it!"

I hushed Edwin, winked at him in my rear view mirror, and mouthed "I've got this."

I looked back at Cecelia and told her, "That would be awesome!! Because you would be the hero! You would have gotten the idea that the phone could teleport and then we'd find it. How amazing!"

She responds cooly, "Well, then, you should check under my pillow."

Wow. I couldn't believe she had taken it! This whole time Edwin knew, though he never had any convincing argument other than "I just know she took it."

This got me thinking about math. Sometimes kids know the answers, though teachers are skeptical. We ask for proof and students say, "I just know it."

The follow-up activity to this true sibling story was to let 5th graders practice being the skeptic and convincer with fractions.

I told students:

You're going to have the chance to be the skeptic and the convincer. You can play the role of Edwin, trying to convince your partner, though hopefully you'll have better justification. Partners, you'll be skeptical. You'll ask clarifying questions until you are convinced.

You will role play, where one student has to convince the other (who is skeptical) that he created a shape that is 1/4 or 1/2 the area of the larger square. Students will alternate convincer and skeptic roles as they create different shapes with the same area.

Finally, sum up the activity in one powerful sentence and answer the question:

Is 1/4 always equal to 1/4? Why or why not? Give examples.

The students were eager to try out their convincing skills as they worked to prove their shapes were 1/4 or 1/2 the size of the larger square. They had totally bought in to the lesson and laughed when they thought about Cecelia's imagination or Edwin's good intuition. And they enjoyed saying hi to Edwin or Cecelia in the hallway, with a smirk as they knew a funny story about them. Students felt a connection with me and my family, and had a great time proving congruent fractions.

There is ample research to support storytelling as a pedagogical strategy, too.

- "In a study conducted by Cliatt and Shaw (1988), the researchers reported that storytelling not only helped participants enhance the language and logic skills of the children but also resulted in the development of positive attitudes towards instruction." And this: "Storytelling is an effective strategy that incorporates the aesthetic ways of knowing into instruction. In addition to improving the academic performance of students in the areas of reading and writing, storytelling also has the ability to enhance the arts in education and motivate children to connect with their learning."

Journal of Cross-Disciplinary Perspectives in Education Vol. 1, No. 1 (May 2008) 36 - 43 42

- "These ideas lead one to consider the storyline approach as an excellent way to help children understand certain ideas about science. For young children a story is not just a powerful tool but a pedagogical necessity. As Egan (1979: p. 2) points out, 'young children require a story form. They require a beginning that sets up an expectation, a puzzle, a problem, or what writers call a sense of tension'. Topics, according to Egan (1988, 1994, 1997), embedded in a context capturing the imagination of the child, should be presented in such a way that the child perceives the conflict between two binary

> opposites (e.g., good and evil, big and little, hope and despair, security and fear)." And this: "If the goal of early childhood science education is to provide opportunities for children to build the foundations for scientific knowledge, then attention should be paid to those characteristics of children's mental life that facilitate this construction process. These characteristics are curiosity/wonder and imagination, and they can both be developed and sustained through exciting stories, in which science concepts and ideas have been embedded. "

Anastasiou, L., Kostaras, N., Kyritsis, E., & Kostaras, A. (2015). The Construction of Scientific Knowledge at an Early Age: Two Crucial Factors. Creative Education, 6, 262-272.

My kids and I recently flew to Florida to visit my mom. At the end of the flight, Cecelia, then 7, exclaimed, "That was the best flight in my whole life!" She wanted to let the pilot know, but our end of the plane was exiting out the back. She went up to a flight attendant and said softly, "I was wondering if you could tell the pilot something. This was the best flight in my whole life!" The flight attendant was a bit caught off-guard, though bent down, looked Cecelia in the eyes, smiled and said, "Of course I can."

A little emotion goes a long way! Marketing companies know it too. You want to get a chance at our purse strings? Start with our heart strings. There are times you might be ready to watch an action movie, or others when a good cry is in order, and still others when a hilarious movie is just the ticket.

I once heard a speaker tell the audience that students should want to buy tickets to our lesson. So step right up, and "sell" tickets to your show!

R.A.C.E. in Action

Let's try out the R.A.C.E concepts. What's an upcoming lesson you'd like to revamp?

Relevancy

Attention Grabber

Challenge

Emotion

Start with the learning target (objective or standard) you'd like students to hit.

Learning Target: The student will identify the main idea in a text.

Relevant Challenging Question:

How could every student share his/ her book in the 35 minutes before lunch?

Attention Grabber: True story from my childhood.

Emotion evoked by: Here's the story:

Boys and girls, I've been hearing you chat with each other about your books and you have some amazing characters! I want to hear about all of them. I remember reading a series of books called The Saddle Club when I was about 9. I loved the books so much that I pretended to be one of the main characters, Stevie. Sometimes, I even signed her name when I wrote letters to my friend! I got to know Stevie so well that I even began talking like her. Have you ever liked a main character that much?

Maybe you're reading a story that I would really like. How could I make sure that I get to hear about everyone's story?"

Elicit responses and guide them to the concept of "main idea."

"Let's try that out! Could we have every student share his/ her book in 35 minutes if we just share the main idea? What steps could we take?"

Brainstorm the possible steps in figuring out the main idea of a text. Give students time to figure out the main idea and the following day, try out the challenge: Can everyone share within 35 minutes (or change up the time frame, maybe you want them to share in groups of 5 and have everyone share in 5 minutes)? Maybe students could find students who have similar main ideas, and they could share together? After hearing all those main ideas, students may be excited to share ideas for what to do next. For example, they could create a Main Idea Wall where the main ideas are written on index cards and posted under various categories (animal characters, genres, chapter books, etc.).

Check out the resource section for more lesson planning templates. Your lessons could become a full-fledged musical like The Greatest Showman! It may sound a bit over-the-top, but that's ok. The only limit is that which you accept and there's no need to limit what you or your students can accomplish!

5

ENGAGEMENT ELIMINATES MISBEHAVIOR

I'm sure you've had the "teacher dream" before. The one where you're in front of the class and everything is out of control. The students won't listen and you feel little, insignificant, and ineffective. You wake up feeling grateful that it was just a dream, though you may carry a little bit of apprehension that the dream could become a reality.

When the time comes and that nightmare inevitably comes true, we all seem to manage. I've used all sorts of classroom management systems: student planners, incentive charts, clips, stoplight colors, and stamps. For me, the most effective management tool has been my teaching itself.

When students are laughing and enjoying a task, incidents of misbehavior disappear. I remember a principal commenting on my third grade students' behavior during a science lesson. He remarked, "You don't even need a behavior system! Your students are so engaged, there are no behaviors to correct."

There are some students, maybe 5-10%, that may have other things going on at home that prevent them from being as engaged. There are always those exceptions, though I believe we can touch every student.

Remember, Michael? I had to really shift my own perspective and let go of my ego. There is no place for power struggles in the classroom. I smirk as I write, because really there's no place for them at home either. Especially with my own two kiddos, who provide me with lots of growth opportunities.

Just this week, Edwin's writing teacher showed me his response to "If I were a bee I would..." The expectation was to respond to the prompt in 5 sentences. He wrote, "If I were a bee I would sting and dye (his spelling)," with an orange crayon. She told him it would be graded and he confidently responded, "I don't care." He clearly wasn't interested in engaging with the prompt any more than that. I was embarrassed and disappointed in him, at first. A teacher's son was refusing to complete his work and follow directions.

I took his paper and told her I'd have him work on it at home. When he got home from school he told me that writing wasn't fun today. I didn't even have to bring it up! He said they had to write about "all these dumb prompts like if I were a bee, or a flower, or a pond. Isn't that stupid?" It turns out he had a few worries in this class - the music was too loud, a boy was acting up (his behavior varied from class to class), social studies was over, and writing about bees and flowers seemed pointless.

While he had trouble explaining which of those things was really bothering him, I got the sense that it was a culmination of all of them. He's a sensitive kid, and, while he came off as rude and non-compliant, I knew he was struggling with other stuff. I asked if he was disrespectful to the teacher and he said, "kind of." We talked about how it's ok to dislike a task, but it's not okay to be disrespectful to the teacher. I asked if he could respond to a different prompt so that he could still complete the assignment, though how about using a different kind of "bee?" "If I were a B-17 bomber, I would..." He enjoys reading about history and planes. As soon as he heard that prompt, he was eager to write about it. I didn't have to beg or bribe him.

I know we can't always give kids a choice about what to write about, namely during state tests. But what if we can provide more choice all those other times? Does the standard measure if students can write about the perspective of a bee, or write to show an understanding of how varying perspectives affect a narrative?

Disengagement is often misdiagnosed as misbehavior.

SOMETHING I really dislike is doing our taxes. I used to procrastinate and then spend hours figuring out all the details. Eventually I hired someone to do them for us. That was a huge relief! I'd so much rather spend my time doing just about anything else, and it was a smart move. Why waste time and energy doing something I dislike when I could be using the strengths in my wheelhouse to write creative lessons?

Kids don't like to waste their time either. It goes back to relevancy - why is this important?

When kids shut down, due to a host of issues we may not see or even be able to understand, it can be tough to turn it around. Giving consequences doesn't necessarily address the situation effectively. We have to get to the root of what's behind the misbehavior. Remember, "A misbehaving child is a discouraged child." (Quote from Jane Nelson in Chapter 1)

I was supporting a teacher who asked a boy to sit in his chair. He refused. He leaned on it, tilted it sideways, squatted on it, and toyed with all the ideas he could do, besides sit in his chair. It was super frustrating to ask him nicely and watch him smirk and flat-out refuse to comply. At this point, he was distracting the other students. I wanted to let the teacher continue with her teaching, so I intervened.

"Craig, are you able to sit in your chair?" I asked him.

"No," he replied curtly.

"How about we go for a quick walk?" I offered.

He looked at me, searching my face to see if he was in trouble. "Why?"

"I want to help you. Mrs. C has asked you to sit in your chair and it looks like you're struggling with it. Can we go for a quick walk so we can chat about what's bothering you?"

"Fine."

During our walk, I learned that he wasn't sleeping well at home. He had quite a few brothers who were either older and loud at night, or they were really young and would wake him up crying. It sounded like there wasn't a lot of structure at bed time, and he shared his time between his mom and dad's houses. I looked at the dark circles under his eyes and saw him as a 4th grade boy who was having a hard time. He was trying to be a tough-guy, and the lack of sleep was really wearing on him.

We brainstormed some ideas to help him both at home and at school - one of which was to allow him time to sleep at school. Sleep is a basic need. We can't (and shouldn't have to) compete with it.

When we returned to the classroom, he found a beanbag to sit on and he finished his work. Now there was a new understanding about his work habits. To get to that point he had to be seen, heard, and supported. The power struggle disappeared. As we checked in with and addressed his needs, he was able to be more productive.

Another quick way to turn around my own kids' behavior is by pointing out an interesting distraction. "Hey guys, check out all the deer grazing in our backyard!" or "Uh-oh, come see what your kitty just caught."

Consider this. You're at an education conference, and the presenter starts by sitting on a stool in front of the room and sharing all the books she's written over the last few years, which sound only the slightest bit interesting. You look back at the session guide to see what this session is supposed to be about: "Sparking Children's Curiosity About Writing." You hope you'll walk away with some helpful strategies for engaging students in the writing process.

As it turns out, the presenter is not an educator and is really only interested in selling her books. She offers a few samples of how she wrote her books using wildlife as the subjects. She speaks in monotone, and you wonder how this conference chooses presenters. The realization sets in that this session is going to be a waste of time, but you're sitting in the middle of the third row. You don't want to be rude and walk out right in front of her, so you sit and pretend to take notes, though you're actually writing your to-do list and checking email. The presenter starts reading aloud another one of her books and you look back at the session guide; there's got to be another great session that you could still catch.

Finally, you've had it. You actually resent the presenter for misleading you, and as she turns to pick up yet another book, you quickly walk out of the room without looking back.

What was missing from the presenter's session? What interfered with your engagement and learning? There's so much!

Teachers are sometimes the worst audience - I speak from both the perspective of a teacher having been in the audience and of a presenter. If teachers sense the presenter has no teaching experience or the information is not useful, the session will be a waste of time. The presenter will have a difficult time keeping teachers engaged.

When the speaker earns our trust, like Michael Bonner does when he speaks, we are at the edge of our seats to hear what great tips he can share next. Michael was a keynote speaker at an NWEA Fusion Conference. Since I'd never heard of him, I was skeptical about what his message would be. Well, he blew my socks off! He opened by sharing his experience teaching 2nd graders in a Carolina elementary, located in a not-so-good part of town. Part of his story included a girl who refused to do any work, got up in his face to sass him, kicked him in the leg (twice), and then proceeded to pull all the books off of his nicely organized bookshelves. Right away, I started to trust him. I realized he's been there, he understands what real-life teaching is like. His speech was incredible, and I ran out to buy his book and stand in line to get it autographed.

Michael was animated, hilarious, authentic, a great story-teller, and quite the teacher. I walked away with pages of useful notes. I posted his quotes on my Facebook page and found great insight for how I wanted to support teachers in my district.

I want to be inspired. Kids want to be inspired too. If you're bored with teaching, your kids will be bored too. What would inspire you? Start there. Baby steps are still steps in the right direction.

Shifting Perspective

My sweetpea kids were arguing in the backseat as I was driving down the highway. Their argument was escalating, and I responded in typical mom fashion. "Keep your hands and feet to yourselves and leave each other alone. Edwin stop hitting her, CC get back over in your spot."

Next thing you know, Cecelia is crying and holding her nose, and it's bleeding all over the back seat. Still driving, and now crazy angry and a tad worried, I grab a roll of paper towels I happened to have in the passenger seat and throw them back to her. I looked for a place to pull over and then I told them both, "You know what? I'm not stopping. You guys want to beat each other up. Go ahead. I don't want to be late for my appointment because I had to clean up my daughter's bloody nose that my own son gave her!" Oh, I was fuming. I did say a few other choice words... certainly not mom of the year material.

I needed to shift my anger because all I wanted to do was give them to another, more patient mom who could raise them better. My kids were both shocked that I didn't stop and help CC. I needed to shift their perspective too, especially my son as he now started to say what a stupid kid he is and that I should just give him away.

I have a few favorite perspective shifters, and it was definitely time to use them. The first one I tried with my kids (and me) was turning on some good music. That was a good start, though not enough at the time. I ended up turning down the music and asked, "Hey Edwin, did you ever come up with a good idea for a craft for the nursing home?" He shook his head but then responded, "Could we paint with them? Maybe we could help them make bracelets?" Cecelia piped up, "We could bring Clover (our miniature horse) in and that would cheer people up." Now our discussion was productive, and it felt good to be planning something that would benefit others. We began thinking about others instead of our anger.

Here are my top 10 techniques for shifting perspective:

1. Listen to music
2. Plan to give
3. Dance
4. Laugh
5. Paint
6. Practice gratitude
7. Breathe (more than a few deep breaths)
8. Journal
9. Color or doodle
10. Exercise

Shifting perspective is also important for us as teachers. Let's take lunch time. Lunch time is precious. Those 20 minutes of uninterrupted, peaceful moments where we take our time enjoying our delicious warm meal....

Ok, so I'm not sure that actually exists for most teachers. And don't get me started about the myth of *uninterrupted daily plan time*!

I remember sitting in meetings at school, where our administrators were reminding teachers to promptly pick students up from specials. None of us really intended on being late picking up our students. Sometimes we had meetings scheduled during our plan time, a parent phone call lasted longer than we expected, we got caught up in answering an email, or the copier kept breaking down, all of which left no time for a bathroom stop. We took advantage of having the students being supervised by the specials teacher and took an extra two minutes to run to the bathroom.

I also remember thinking that the administrators don't understand what we do or value our time. Resentment was growing. It was fueled as I ate lunch with colleagues and attended union meetings after school.

Here's the thing: I've worked closely with many administrators over the past few years, and you know what I discovered? Most administrators don't have a plan time either, or even have time for lunch! I'm honestly not sure how the administrators keep up with their staff, parents, and students. And keep in mind, the emails, phone calls, and visits they get aren't typically pleasant - whether from parents or teachers!

It's easy to find blame in others. To become the victim of state mandates. To judge co-workers who leave early (one school even had a term for this, "the purse club," for those women who have their purse in hand just after the dismissal bell rings). To feel like the administrators keep adding to our already overflowing plates. To consider getting out of teaching altogether.

I don't like admitting it, but I was there. Full of negativity, blame, and resentment. Ew.

After years of wanting out of education, I had that opportunity. I was teaching half-time and running a nutrition practice on the side. I had grown my practice and was ready to take the next steps to have a full time practice. I was about to invest in a mastermind coaching group that suggested it would provide massive support to grow my business. Joining this mastermind would require me to choose a focus: teaching or nutrition. My chance to leave teaching was right in front of me.

And... I didn't take it.

I contemplated my choices. Even though I was passionate about nutrition and helping my clients heal all sorts of digestive issues, I realized that my favorite part about that role was coaching. I enjoyed teaching my clients about new ways to eat and take care of themselves, and I got really excited when they reached their goals. The experience I had acquired in nutrition coaching had actually made me a better, more reflective teacher. I learned how to listen, how to connect with others, and how to help them grow in areas they didn't know were possible.

The thing is, I had done a lot of soul-searching the year before. I had quit a highly sought after, well-paid teaching position at a top Ohio school. My new, part-time position was at a smaller, rural school closer to home. On paper, the pros/cons of leaving didn't add up; I would be working more hours and making considerably less money. However, I would be closer to home and teaching in my children's school.

I chatted with my husband, mom, sister, dad, and teaching friends to seek advice. In the end it turned out to be a heart-based decision. It felt right. And three years later, it's still proved to be the right decision.

If we're not sure why we teach, or our why has become tarnished over the years, it's time to either consider another profession or dig our heels in and commit to the life-changing profession that often chooses us.

A COACH HELPED me brainstorm my vision. If I could wave a magic wand and create the perfect role for me, what would I be doing? When I considered the question, having a successful nutrition practice wasn't part of that vision. Teaching is in my bones. It's the reason I'm on this earth. Even if I'd been considering quitting for the last few years, I realized I belong in the education realm. I wanted to support teachers. I wanted to help them feel better about the amazing job they do. I wanted to help them feel more valued. I wanted to make their jobs easier so they could focus on the things that matter most.

For me to stay in education, my perspective had to shift. I revisited my why: Why do I teach? Our **why** should be our anchor.

The very next day, I printed off my vision. I was feeling a bit re-inspired at my decision to stay in education as I ran into our new superintendent in the hallway.

He asked, "Can I walk with you?"

"Sure." What else was I going to say?

"What are your goals? What do you hope to accomplish?"

Funny. I literally had just figured this out the day before.

We got to my classroom and continued our conversation.

"I want to coach teachers. I want to make their jobs easier. I want to lead professional development. I want to reach even more teachers."

He listened and nodded. "Let's make that happen."

"Ok!" I replied and we began brainstorming what this coaching role would look like.

Wow. I figured out what my heart wanted, and the universe responded. When we get clear about what our goals are - goals that are in alignment with our heart and soul - new doors open. It's almost as if this alignment creates this magnetic flow of energy that attracts the components we need to make the goals happen.

While there are still hundreds of things I'd like to change in the teaching world, I'm not venting about them. I'm looking for solutions. My intention is to be of service. I tend to be pretty enthusiastic, especially when I'm excited about something. So much so that one of my colleagues calls me, "Jen 'Curb your Enthusiasm' Molitor."

I question things more out of curiosity than from a need to get my own way. I attended a fabulous workshop at Marzano Research last March, and the presenter, Tammy Heflebower (you might recognize her name from the foreword), shared that when she works with schools, she often says, "I promise not everyone will get their own way. So at some point, we need to build a bridge and get over it."

At some point, we need to make that decision. Committing to a career filled with negativity and resentment cannot be very fulfilling.

From 'Overwhelmed' to 'I love my job!'

1. Find your Why
2. Choose (to teach or not)
3. Commit
4. Do one small thing daily to support your commitment (see the upcoming table for possible ideas)
5. Find a colleague who can hold you accountable and support your endeavor
6. Reflect often to refine your commitment

Here's one secret for feeling fulfilled. At the end of every day, find 3 things that went well or that you're proud of. The more you look for, the more amazing things you'll see. This practice actually rewires the brain to look for more successes, and in turn will help you achieve more successes.

Another tip. If you've done your very best, and at the end of the day that doesn't feel good enough, make a quick list of three things that would have helped you. Then reach out and get support.

I Choose to Teach!

Ideas for Supporting your Commitment to Teach

- Write your "Why" with fun markers and laminate it.
- Schedule a self-care time slot once a month for the rest of the school year. (Think massage, pedicure, hike, movie, personal day, pet a puppy, read a novel, etc.)
- Set goals for the year - I recommend one for teaching and the other for personal growth.
- Create a marble jar for yourself. Every time you do something you're proud of, drop a marble in the jar. When it's full, celebrate! Think of it as filling your bucket. This is something you and your colleagues could do together.
- Bring fresh flowers to school to put on your desk.
- Observe a colleague.
- Listen to an inspiring podcast on the way to work.
- Attend a conference.
- Incorporate a one minute mindfulness moment in your day (with or without students).
- Write a thank you note to someone who has inspired or supported you.
- Create a feedback box for students to share what they like and ideas for improvements. Don't worry, in my experience students tend to give honest, enlightening, useful feedback.
- Share your goals for the year with your families. They can be so supportive!

What Kids Need Most

One Monday morning, I got one of those lengthy parent emails from a 5th grade parent that warranted a phone call rather than the standard quick email reply. The email was about one of my most thoughtful, genuinely caring students, I'll call him Eric. Through tears, the mom wrote about how much her son was going through. Eric was gifted, academics came easily, he won many contests, and had even been interviewed on the news. He was well spoken and charming, and he seemed to have everything in his favor.

However, there was so much going on inside. He was dealing with kids calling him "ugly," football players calling him a "grass fairy" because he was an avid soccer player, a gym teacher suggesting he carry the lighter pieces of equipment (since he plays soccer), and feeling that everyone was against him.

Eric's mom and I chatted for about an hour. Eric hadn't wanted her to talk with the principal or get anyone in trouble. His mom didn't know what to do, so they had made a compromise to reach out to me.

When my students came in after recess, I brought them to the carpet for a chat. I told them that as they get older, friends start to change and sometimes kids do mean things without realizing how their words and actions affect others.

Everyone was so receptive, and they started sharing their own stories. Eric openly shared many of the stories that his mom told me about. As a group we talked about tolerance, standing up for yourself, talking about concerns with someone they trust, forgiveness, that it's ok to feel icky stuff and it's possible to choose to find a path through it. A few made comments like, "This is exactly what I needed today." Another student told me, "You're kinda like a mom to us." I told them I hope to be a better person today than I was the day before. That's how we grow.

These kids had so much on their minds! As we chatted, they brought up politics, gay rights, abortion, gun control, and freedom of speech. I definitely was careful as we touched on such delicate topics. I honored their thinking and brought them back to things we can change. My goal was to empower them and to let them know that while we may want to change the world, we can't change everyone. And even though we may disagree with another's choices, like cussing at recess and making fun of others because of their preferences, we also need to practice tolerance and grace.

I think it was good for all of them to hear that other people are dealing with stuff too.

It took a solid hour to discuss their feelings and brainstorm strategies to support them. Students felt listened to, they felt they *mattered.* As teachers, we focus so much on lesson planning, assessment, and finding the perfect resources, and rightly so! While academics are the meat of our job, I propose the other 50% should be true rapport building. There are some days when academics need to sit on the back burner. Students are people first. It can be easy to get caught up in the demands of teaching and get into that "teacher = authority" mentality.

Kids are carrying around major stuff: stuff we could never guess, stuff we could never imagine, and stuff we tend to brush aside. One student told me, "My teacher just tells me to go sit down if I ever share a concern." Even by middle school, students are dealing with the pressures of depression, addiction, and suicide.

I can't over emphasize this enough - we NEED to slow down and make time for students. Make eye contact. Truly listen. Model how to be resilient and kind. Model how to deal with changes to the schedule. Model how to receive feedback. Kids know when we're authentic.

As teachers, we always hear about the "problem child." It's as if we get to choose who we like, who we believe in, who we assume won't ever catch up, who doesn't deserve to get those extra smiles. The thing is, we've been gifted this role, one that should be done from a place of integrity. We get the opportunity to shape these students' lives. We get to be the person they look up to.

Imagine you needed a major heart surgery and the prerequisite was to spend the week at the surgeon's facilities to prepare. You noticed the doctor ate 3 donuts and drank a Red Bull at breakfast. For lunch she ate a Big Mac, fries, and a large Coke. You noticed her snacking on Oreos around 2pm and couldn't help but glare as she ate an entire row and washed it down with another Red Bull. She treated her staff as if they were little more than servants. You overheard her complain about another patient, who developed complications after his surgery.

How do you feel? Reassured? Hopeful? Your life is literally in her hands, but you wouldn't feel comfortable telling her any requests or preferences you have. You'd feel un-empowered in regards to your own health, stifled and shot down when you're met with eye rolls and yawning. On the flip side, if your surgeon is warm, compassionate, understanding, patient, and friendly, you might feel you've got a partnership.

Good teaching isn't enough. Our kids deserve more. They deserve to be seen, heard, and understood. They deserve our compassion, patience, and authenticity.

Remember, you can give a student lunch money, greet him in the morning, and give him an extra pat on the back when he's working hard, and he *still* may not feel he matters. Remember Maslow's Hierarchy of needs; without safety and a feeling of belonging, learning is much harder, if not outright impossible. We've got to do more to connect with our students.

If you were meant to be an educator, you get it. You're always striving to grow, to be better for kids. Not everyone has teaching in their DNA, and that's ok. I'd encourage those people to find a job they're better suited for.

Your authenticity, compassion, and drive to be awesome are beacons of light to your district. Stand tall. Walk proudly. You are a teacher.

If I had to work an office job all day, I'd be bored and grumpy. I could be highly skilled in my computer work, though my effectiveness would not be as great because I wasn't 100% all in. I'd be going through the motions and doing the bare minimum. I tend to be highly ambitious and a perfectionist, but those traits seem to be crowded out by disengagement and boredom.

Teaching is not easy, it's not a job. Teaching is a calling, a way of life, and a soul's purpose.

Teaching is a superpower, and you get the opportunity to be a superhero to all the students who pass through your door.

BEYOND STUDENT RELATIONSHIPS

Part 3

6

PARENTS ARE PEOPLE TOO

I remember my first year of teaching, sitting in a meeting (it'd probably be called a Response to Intervention meeting nowadays, but back then we called it a "Problem Solving" meeting), and Stephanie, the mom, was upset. My teaching partner and I, along with the school counselor, a support educator, and psychologist, were at the table with her. We were discussing her son's difficulties with reading, although he was progressing nicely according to our data. My partner had been teaching for a few years, so I often let her take the lead on meetings. She was adamant that Stephanie's son was doing well and that she wasn't seeing anything out of the ordinary. I, too, could attest to his success in my room. The meeting was brought to a close because he was meeting all the benchmarks, though I felt there was something more we could/should do. I could feel the passion and concern Stephanie was expressing, however, there was this collective feeling that Stephanie was overbearing or pushing too much, almost like teachers know best and we have to hold our ground. *'There's no caving in to the demands of pushy parents.'*

I remember hesitating in my explanations and giving Stephanie warm smiles. I wanted her to know that I heard her concerns and that, even though I didn't understand them, I was willing to dig a little more. Fast forward a few years and she sends in an IEP to school with a note that said something like, "See. I told you Brian has learning difficulties. Mrs. Molitor, I know you understood." She circled the diagnosis, something I still have never seen or heard before about a specific disability with how the eyes track the words on a page. This was one convicted mama! She knew there was something interfering with her child's acquisition of skills, and even though she didn't get the support she was looking for that year, she was able to advocate for her son. I felt conflicted. On one hand, I felt badly that our meeting hadn't gone that well for her, and on the other, I felt a little relief that she had felt my compassion.

Somewhere along our development as experienced teachers, we learn to roll our eyes when parents do things differently or, God-forbid, the parents take their kids out of school for a week to go on a Disney trip. *Don't they realize how important school is?!* Now that I'm a mom, I have a different perspective on school. Of course school is important, but just this past year, I took my kids out of school for two days to visit my mom, who moved 20 hours away. To me, spending quality time with their grandma was worth missing two days of school. Sometimes kids need a break from school, whether it's to catch up on sleep due to a demanding sports schedule or because a relative is in town.

I propose a team approach with parents, regardless of differing philosophies. We have to meet in the middle, though yes, there are some parents who do not have their child's best interest in mind. For those tricky situations, we can do our best to love the student, even though he may imitate the inappropriate actions of his parents.

When teachers team up with parents, the impact we make on students is greater. A compilation of research from Anne T. Henderson finds the following:

For example, teacher outreach to parents results in strong, consistent gains in student performance in both reading and math. Effective outreach practices include meeting face to face, sending learning materials home, and keeping in touch about progress. Workshops for parents on helping their children at home are linked to higher reading and math scores. Schools with highly rated partnership programs make greater gains on state tests than schools with lower-rated programs.

-From A New Generation of Evidence: The Family is Critical to Student Achievement, by Anne T. Henderson and Nancy Berla (Washington, DC: Center for Law and Education, 1994) and A New Wave of Evidence: The Impact of School, Family and Community Connections on Student Achievement, by Anne T. Henderson and Karen L. Mapp (Austin, TX: Southwest Educational Development Laboratory, 2002 – in press).

As we consider making compromises with parents, we've got to be careful about how we talk about them when they're not around, too. I learned early on that teachers don't like having a whole bunch of parent emails, and phone calls were even worse, especially if they were questioning an assignment or classroom policy. I saw teachers cringe if their message light was on, and if I got a tricky email where the mom sounded upset with my decision, I would dread having to respond. Not because I didn't like the parent, but I felt defensive that they were questioning me, I worried that maybe I did do something wrong, and deep down, I might have worried that I could be fired.

I remember one mom called in because her son came home from school with a broken leg. He came in from recess hopping and told my teaching partner that he fell and his leg hurt. He was hopping back and forth on both legs so she figured he was ok and sent him to the nurse for ice. He came back to class and finished the day without complaining. We found out the next day, in the message from his mom, that the boy had broken his leg! Although we both were concerned for him, we felt confident that we had done the right thing by sending him to the nurse. Should the mom be mad? I probably would be! Those are tough calls to make.

I recommend that teachers do three things when a student gets hurt (obviously in the event of something life threatening, you should call 911). First, really check in with how the student is feeling. We might ask, "How bad is the pain on a scale of 1-10? Have you ever injured this leg (arm, finger, etc.) before? If the pain doesn't get better or you think we should call your mom, will you let me know?" It's really important to let children feel pain, express how it feels, and understand that pain is usually very intense at first and then subsides a bit as we breathe and time passes. Once kids learn that the pain does go away, they're more likely to rebound quicker next time. When we dismiss their pain, we're sending the message that either it's not ok to feel hurt, or we just don't care.

Second, quickly document the essentials of the conversation, even on a post-it, so you have something concrete to refer back to. It covers your tail, and it can boost your memory later. It's impossible to remember all the conversations and decisions we make in one day, especially after a few days have passed.

Lastly, it would be a compassionate touch to send a quick email to the parent. Something like,

Hi Mrs. Smith,

I hope Charlie's finger is feeling better! He hurt it catching a football at recess today. The pain improved after applying an ice pack and he didn't complain the rest of the day.

Sincerely,

Mrs. M

Those little emails take just a minute to send, though they mean the world to a parent.

Our role as teacher does not mean that we know everything, like we're out to prove that we know what's best for every single student. Just like parenting works best when both parents are on the same page, the same goes for teaching the child. Ideally, teachers and parents would have mutual respect for each other to collaborate on student-centered decisions. Teachers have to navigate 25-30 different personalities in the classroom, another 30 or so of their colleagues, and upwards of 60 parent personalities!

From our end, as long as we reflect that our decisions aren't driven by our ego (out to prove someone else wrong) or defensiveness, and that our decisions were made from a kind place, we'll be ahead of the curve.

7

PLEASING PARENTS WITHOUT BEING A PUSHOVER

I think a course in communication, especially with parents, should be included in teacher education degrees. Teachers often find themselves able to connect really well with kids, but communication with their parents is a whole different story. I've heard teachers say, "If I could just do my job and not have to interact with the parents, that would be perfect."

Ideally we should connect with parents in a way that encourages two-way respect and admiration for what we both do. When we connect this way, we build rapport with parents so they are able to trust us completely.

The 5 Essential C's to Parent Partnerships

Confidence

Parents are more relaxed when they feel assured that their child is in good hands. As a teacher, you have passion, dedication, and commitment to teaching and reaching your students. Own it! You were hired as a teacher based on your education, your teaching heart, and your energy. Parents are looking for answers that you most likely have!

Can you imagine your husband, your dad, or a friend who majored in business taking over your classroom for the day? Even with sub plans? No way! You've got teaching in your bones, and beyond that, you've acquired some mega skills, strategies, and techniques that make you quite the expert. We're not perfect and we may not have all the answers, but that is okay. It's better to tell a parent that you're not sure, but will find out, rather than tell them something you're not sure is true.

Share success stories with parents to support your experience. For example, I spoke with a parent who wanted to discuss her 2nd grade son's poor spelling grades. I told her that Andrew was very bright and that spelling is simply a memorization skill. I wasn't worried about his spelling grade, I was worried about him not growing in other areas. I was pushing him in class to reach farther; he wasn't comfortable with this. In my experience, I found that some students don't want to try activities that are too difficult because they're used to things being easy, and/ or they don't want to make a mistake. I told her we should both encourage him and praise his effort, not his grades. I suspected he was gifted, and when we got testing results at the end of the year, she called me up to thank me. Andrew had received a qualifying score for superior cognitive identification. She realized that shifting our focus from arbitrary grades to effort and perseverance was more rewarding for both of them.

There's no need to "sell" what you do to parents. They simply want to see their child succeed, to get the support they need. So speak their language, confidently, with authenticity and integrity. Even if you have a hunch or a feeling in your gut, share that with parents. While it may not be the science you're looking for, gut decisions are often right on.

Also, remember that confidence doesn't equal perfection, and perfection has no place in education. You can be confident and still have a lesson that flops, that's totally okay!

Be careful to not compare your worst teaching day to the best teaching day of your favorite mentor. It'd be like me comparing my sweet little 15 year old Arabian horse's speed to a young 3-year old thoroughbred colt in training for the Derby. I once heard a 4th grader say she's the shortest person in the whole school (K-5). "See?" she said boldly as she stood next to the tallest boy in her class. The same is true in teaching.

If you compare yourself to the tallest person, you can't help but come up short.

EACH YEAR I choose a focus word. Something for me to cultivate throughout the year. The first word I chose was "confidence," because I wasn't feeling very confident. By the end of the year, I couldn't remember why I chose that word. Setting the intention to be more confident is a powerful way to start. Ultimately, act as if you are confident. Walk confidently. Speak confidently. Adopt a new mantra, "I am confident. I am strong. I am powerful."

Try to balance on one leg (maybe tree pose?) and say, "I can't balance. I'm not good at this," and see what happens. Then try the same pose while repeating the new mantra, "I am confident. I am strong. I am powerful."

I've got one more strategy for you. Amy Cuddy, a social psychologist and award-winning Harvard lecturer, shares the power of using our body language to create positive outcomes in our lives in her 2012 Ted Talk. She suggests that standing in a "powerful pose" before an important meeting or interview can actually improve our performance (Amy Cuddy | TEDGlobal 2012 | June 2012). Her talk is definitely worth the time to listen.

Here's a quick recap to build confidence:

1. Why do you teach? Let your "why" be your anchor. Being able to teach is a gift. Own it!!
2. Don't compare your worst lesson to the National Teacher of the Year's best lesson ever.
3. Choose "Confidence" as your focus word for the year.

4. "I am confident. I am strong. I am powerful."
5. Powerful poses

Communication

I've written a lot of class newsletters in my years in the classroom. I'm sure I wrote something like, "In math we're learning two digit by two digit multiplication and dividing two-digit dividends by one-digit divisors." Of course I know what I'm talking about, but do the parents? I've seen so many newsletters that share, "We'll complete Chapter 3 in math this week and learn about the states in social studies." Chapter 3 probably doesn't mean much to parents and what specifically are they learning about the states - capitals, location, physical features, etc.?

Parents want to know what's going on in THEIR language. They may not know all the lingo: IEP, 504, WEP, RTI, DARE, CARE, DRA, AIR, MAP, etc., so don't use it. It's actually harder than you might think. We use our teacher lingo all day. For example, we might share with parents, "On Tuesday, we'll compare our winter MAP scores to the baseline RIT scores from the fall, and we'll use the learning continuum to set new goals for students' WEPs." Do the parents really know what any of that means? They might figure out that their child will be setting new goals, but how and what does that mean for their child?

Newsletter Tips

- What if your students helped create each newsletter? I bet that would get parents to read them more often.
- What do parents really NEED to know about your class that week?
- Include the students as much as possible: pictures of students, examples of exemplary work, student created sections of the newsletter.
- What about using a simple website as your newsletter?
- What about a personalized newsletter? Each student could fill out a template (which may have important dates, a lunch menu, etc. already included) each week to let his/her own

parents know what she did in each subject, what she needs more practice on, what she's proud of, etc.

What Parents Really Want to Know

- Is my child being challenged? How?
- Is my child behind? How will you help? What can I do?
- What's your homework policy?
- Will you love and take care of my kid?
- Does my child have friends?
- What will it take for my child to do well in your class? What does doing well look like?

I highly recommend offering curriculum nights. This is a great place to share the results parents can expect and when to expect them. They don't necessarily need to know ALL the steps you'll take to get those results. Sharing what your goals and expectations are for the beginning of the year gives parents clarity in knowing what their child should be doing to show they're on target.

You might share a sample of math problems students should know coming into 2nd grade as well as those problems they will be expected to know by the end of the first quarter. Parents don't typically understand what a DRA (Developmental Reading Assessment) level is or what it means if their child is reading at an H. **When we speak our parents' language, they feel at ease and their trust in us is magnified.**

Including a "Question and Answer" area on your newsletter might be a good addition. Think about the most frequently asked questions you get from parents and put a few in your newsletter each week to be proactive.

You might offer a few content area workshops throughout the year. I usually offer seminars on mindset, which led me to being viewed as an expert in that area. This builds credibility and confidence. What are some areas where you are well-versed? What workshops could your students lead for parents?

Communication Builders:

1. Share your simple, straight-forward, clear, and loving philosophy for teaching.
2. Speak the parents' language.
3. Eliminate acronyms from newsletters and conversations.
4. Offer curriculum nights or workshops throughout the year to share your expertise.
5. Upgrade your newsletters.

Compassion

Ding. You hear the email come through on your phone and glance at the clock - 11pm, who is emailing this late?! But you already have a hunch. It's Dylan's mom. Despite your best judgement, your curiosity nudges you to read the late-night email from a parent of one of your 2nd graders, who has already emailed you six times this week.

Mrs. M,

Dylan came home last night upset about his spelling test. He said you read the words too fast and didn't call on him when he raised his hand for you to slow down. I've been in your room during spelling tests and you do read the words quickly. Can you please re-administer the spelling test tomorrow morning @ 9:25am. He has a dentist appointment so I'll be picking him up right @ 10am. That should give you plenty of time. I've also revised the paper you offer for spelling tests. (See attached) The lines are too close together and a bit blurry.

In addition, I would like to schedule a meeting with you this Friday @ 7am. Dylan is complaining that he's bored in math and I'd like to discuss options for providing him with 5th grade level math work. I'll send you the calendar invite in just a few minutes.

One more thing. Dylan got a new pair of shoes - white of all things! He'll be wearing those tomorrow. If it's muddy outside, can you please let him stay in for recess?

I appreciate it! He runs around so much I'm worried he'll ruin the shoes in one day.

Sincerely,

Mrs. Kirkpatrick

Conjures up some lovely memories, right? I'm sure you've gotten similar emails where the parent emails about her child's concerns without asking for your perspective and then *gently* suggests another option to ensure her child's success. She also manages to schedule another conference with you two hours before school starts, again without checking in with you, while hinting that you're not meeting his needs in math. She wants to talk about 5th grade options?! When he doesn't finish his grade level work because he's running around the classroom? And the shoes thing. That just takes the cake.

Your next conversation is with the teacher across the hall. "Seriously!" you tell her, "Did Dylan explain that he was lying on the floor during part of our spelling test and that he tied another girl's shoelaces together in between words?! I think he had plenty of time to write the words, had he been in his seat."

You are fuming. Insulted. Disrespected. Offended.

I get it. I've been there. Many times.

It's hard to show compassion when you feel angry and unappreciated. You brainstorm responses to her that are polite yet firm, while thinking, "No I won't use your stupid lined paper, no I won't 're-administer' the spelling test, I'm not meeting @ 7am, and your son needs to go outside to play."

I'm going to recommend some tips for responding to Dylan's mom so that you can still sleep at night.

#1: "Be kind. Always. For everyone you meet is fighting a battle you know nothing about." I'd love to give credit for the author of this quote, though it appears many people have claimed it.

What if I told you that Dylan's mom was abandoned when she was 4, in foster care for three years after that, and after being adopted for only three years, lost her mother to cancer? She put herself through college and was told she would never be able to have a baby. She battled breast cancer at 35 and two years later, miraculously, she had Dylan. She's had a lot going on in her life! Dylan is her pride and joy, her hope for a better childhood. He represents newness and the chance to cultivate a happy family.

Does she want him to have every opportunity possible? You bet. Will she advocate for him every step of the way? Yuppers. Does she know what a day in the life of a teacher is like? Nope. When I became a teacher my mom told me, "Man, I think I need to send your teachers a thank-you gift. I had no idea how hard they work. I never said thank you or sent in a card or gift."

The majority of people have no idea what we do. I remember my best friend from high school coming to visit me during my first year of teaching. My third graders had packed up and I was reading aloud on the carpet before we were dismissed. After school she said, "It's so cool that you're being paid to read books to kids!" Sigh.

Pretend every parent has a similar story to Dylan's mom. Give them some grace. We can never truly know what they are battling.

#2: "Forgiveness is a "greater understanding" that does not occur instantaneously; it is the end result of a choice to NOT be held hostage by self-judgment or resentment towards another and to begin the healing process. True forgiveness, therefore, requires intention, attention, and time." -Megyn Blanchard

We can hold on to stuff forever. Yes, there's the worksheets, extra pencils (oh, wait, we never have extra pencils), resource books, posters, and lessons that we just can't seem to part with. But we also hold onto the resentment towards parents and kids that have offended us. It often seems to help when we vent to our teaching partner, though while it's okay to chat about, at some point we need to forgive the parents and move on.

Intentional Forgiveness

1. Allow yourself to feel anger, insult, and other icky emotions.
2. Pay attention, you might feel that emotion show up as a physical sensation, like a twinge in your shoulder or a tightness in your chest.
3. Turn your attention to the physicality of the emotion and breath into that spot, allowing it to be there.
4. Visualize the emotions moving through you and out into space.
5. Breath in forgiveness.

When you remember the parent's email or harsh words, also remind yourself, "Oh, that's right. I forgave her." The negative strength of the emotions will lessen over time, as will the resentment that can build up in your body.

#3: Compose your response from this new place, one of compassion, grace, and forgiveness. A phone call can be a better option, if you're grounded. Though an email could go something like this,

Hi Mrs. Kirkpatrick,

Thank you for letting me know about Dylan's shoes. My daughter once insisted on wearing her new white shirt to art class on a day they were painting. Thankfully we were able to get the paint off! I have recess duty this week so Dylan won't be able to stay inside. You might allow him to bring a change of shoes for recess. He is full of energy during class, so I definitely want to give him time to run around outside.

I am glad you emailed. I wanted to fill you in on Dylan's day yesterday. He struggled a bit during the spelling test. In between words, he would lie on the floor. It turns out he was tying another student's shoelaces together. We chatted about the safety concerns of both being on the floor and tying shoelaces together.

I imagine he missed those two words because his attention was on the shoelaces more than spelling. I do want to give an accurate picture of his ability to spell those words versus his behavior. I have time on Thursday to retest him on those two words and I'll let you know how he does. (You could thank her for the revised spelling paper or let it go.)

Unfortunately, I'm not able to meet this Friday at 7am. I'd like to invite a few other colleagues to our meeting so that we can get a comprehensive plan together to meet Dylan's needs. I'll check in with them and get back to you with some dates by this Friday. Dylan has been excited to share his math thinking with us so I'll continue to stretch him during our math stations.

I appreciate your willingness to work together. It's so important to me that Dylan enjoys school!

Warmly,

Mrs. M

Compassion Builders

How can you show your heart-based teaching philosophy with your parents?

1. What would it take for you to make parents smile and think, "She's such a great teacher?" Do that. Within reason, of course.
2. Write positive notes home. Choose one student to write one quick sentence each day or at least one quick note each week. Jot down a quick schedule so that every student gets at least one. I start with a basic outline, though if a student helps a friend who dropped all his books, I might switch him on the schedule, or write two notes that day. Notes don't necessarily have to be about catching a student doing something good. See the resource section at the end of the book for a few ideas to get you started.
3. Make sure parents know you love your job. They know this by the comments you write on student papers, by the energy in your voice, and by your interactions on a daily basis.
4. Give parents and students the benefit of the doubt. None of us are perfect, though we're all in the business of growing. Practice grace with your students, your parents, and most of all, with yourself.
5. Intentionally forgive each student and parent for their misbehavior every day. Make that a 30 second routine on the

way home. To amplify the effect, begin by forgiving yourself for the lesson that flopped, for reprimanding a student a bit too harshly, or for not being perfect. ♡

Collaboration

If parents get the impression that you don't encourage their involvement, at least as far as the school day is concerned, they'll fret more. Remember, parents want to know that their children are safe, loved, learning, and happy. Reassure parents of these things often. One of my son's teachers sent me a quick video of him dancing at an assembly. He was clearly having fun and it made my day to see him showing off his dance moves - and in front of many other 4th grade classes! I wouldn't have been as touched if she sent me an email letting me know the class reviewed for the science quiz this week.

Let parents know that you want their support, questions, feedback, etc. because that will support your teaching efforts. Parents need to know that the work they do at home is just as important as the work you do at school. If a parent wants to pull her son out of school to go to the zoo with her aunt, be graceful in your response. What a great opportunity for the student!

In Don Miguel Ruiz's book, The Four Agreements, he shares the following four pieces of wisdom.

#1: *Be impeccable with your word.*

If you tell parents you'll update them in two weeks, be sure you put that on your calendar. When you talk about Johnny outside the school day, use the same words you would if his parents were around. This habit builds integrity and strengthens your rapport with students and parents. Your colleagues will also find you more trustworthy. You know that one teacher who never seems to say a harsh word about anyone? You can be that teacher.

#2: *Don't take anything personally.*

This one really made me sit down and think. When things frustrate us, they're triggers for something that needs to be healed within us. I can choose to take things personally or not. It's easy to blame others for making us angry, but when we take ownership of our feelings, we experience more growth and reduce the number of things that trigger us.

I bought a 12 pack of frozen hamburgers for an upcoming family get together. When I got home, I asked my 7-year old daughter to put them in the freezer downstairs. Well the following day I went down stairs and saw the box of hamburgers in a laundry basket on the basement floor. I picked them up and realized those were the hamburgers that were supposed to go in the freezer- and now that they'd been out for 24 hours, they were probably no good. My family would be coming in just a few hours for a grill out and we'd be short 12 hamburgers!

I ran upstairs to yell at CC. "Why didn't you put them in the freezer? Now they're ruined. Why can't you just listen and follow directions? This is wasteful!"

My husband heard and he lost it. He yelled at her even more, "I'm sick of this. Sick of you and your brother being lazy. Not paying attention. This is ridiculous! Now we're wasting food. Your mom and I work so hard to take care of this place and you do things like this."

I was angry, but whoa, I didn't expect him to lose it like that too! When I heard him, I calmed down and saw the 7-year old little girl who messed up. She didn't mean to be wasteful. She might have set them down to pet her cat and forgot about the hamburgers. Who knows? The thing is, my husband and I both took her mistake personally - for me it was a reflection of poor parenting, a failure on my part. For my husband, I realize it stemmed back to his childhood. He has shared that his family didn't have a lot growing up. I think wasting 12 perfectly good hamburgers reminded him of how his family struggled. It may have also triggered something about being able to provide for his family.

I took CC aside and pulled her onto my lap. I gave her a big hug and said, "I love you sooooo much. I'm sorry we both got so angry. Do you remember why you didn't put the hamburgers in the freezer?" She shook her head. Gently, I told her, "It's ok. We all mess up. Do you think you can try listening a little better from now on?" She nodded. I explained why I thought Daddy was upset and then we made plans to make a cake for our family gathering.

This can happen when students misbehave in the classroom. We can take a student's misbehavior personally and begin to resent them. This interferes with both rapport and learning!

So when you get a parent email that makes you cringe, or you get defensive, remember: it's a trigger for something else you need to work through. Try not to be mad at the parent or student, but be grateful for the opportunity to heal this trigger within you.

*Disclaimer: This one isn't easy! Learning is a process. The first step is to be aware and recognize when something is triggering you.

#3: *Don't make assumptions.*

As long as we're polite and being honest from a good, heart-based place, honesty is best. If our feedback triggers something in the other person, remember: it's not our fault they have those triggers. It's something they can work through (though they may not know how!).

#4: *Always do your best.*

"Always do your best. What you plant now, you will harvest later."
-Og Madino

Recently, I interviewed for our middle school principal position. This decision shocked most people because I had never been interested in any principal position, and I hadn't acquired my principal licensure yet. I had a week to prepare for the performance task interview and create a principal portfolio. I spent hours researching, printing, rehearsing, and putting together my presentation.

After the interview, I felt a huge sense of relief. I had completed the task, had kept breathing, and didn't throw up... and I felt that I had done a pretty good job. Given my experience and the time given to prepare, I had done my best. If I had to do it over, there's not much I would change. I didn't get the position, but I had done my best and I felt really good about that.

Commitment

I'm going to assume a few things about you:

1. You're the type of person who doesn't give up on a kid.
2. You're committed to figuring out the best way to support a child.
3. You chose to teach AND teaching seemed to choose you - your career feels like a calling.

I sat in on an interview the other day. The interviewee, Emma, responded to questions with good answers. For example, I asked, "What draws you to the teaching profession?" And honestly, I can't remember her answer. I remember I nodded because it was a good answer. Something I agreed with, though nothing that made me 100% sure she was meant for teaching.

Later on in the interview Emma shared a story about a 2nd grade student in an inner city school who was ostracized by his teachers and his peers. DJ sat at a desk away from all the other tables in the far corner of the room. It was clear that he wasn't included often.

Since it was a temporary field placement, she wasn't in charge of the classroom or even teaching a lesson. Emma asked the teacher about DJ, and the teacher responded that he didn't do his work, distracted others, and was a handful. Emma was disappointed in the response and decided to get to know the little boy.

She found out the little boy was just placed with his grandfather, who struggled to make ends meet. DJ told her he was out late the other night. He was walking around the block offering to take out the garbage for neighbors to earn money to buy his grandfather a birthday present. We let out an "awww" as she continued. She helped DJ brainstorm other ways to earn money and eventually helped him get a present for his grandpa. She wrapped up her story with, "I just want to keep making an impact on kids' lives."

Emma had our attention. She spoke with tears in her eyes and all seven of us became aware of her passion for kids. We had discovered her "why." One of the teacher's even pointed at her and said, "That. That story. That's what you share when someone asks you why you want to be a teacher."

If parents only hear generic statements from you, they'll have trouble connecting with and trusting you. For example, I found the following in a google search for a welcome letter:

I hope you have had a great summer and are ready to get back to school and LEARN! I look forward to meeting you. I am confident you will have a fantastic year. I have been busy planning lessons and activities that will challenge you to grow both academically and socially. You are now a member of "Team Blue!" Remember, Open House is scheduled for Friday, Aug. 23 from 6-7:30 p.m. You may meet me, visit our classroom, and get acquainted with your classmates at this time. The first day of school is Monday, Aug. 26. We will begin the year by creating our classroom's Social Contract, reviewing important rules and procedures, and evaluating your Reading and Spelling skills. A supply list is printed on the back of this letter.

The letter talks about a "Social Contract," reviewing rules (which happens every. single. year.), and reading and spelling skills evaluations. The teacher also shares "I am confident you will have a fantastic year!" which is positive and cheery.

Do parents know this teacher is committed to making sure their children will be loved, seen, and valued? Think about your why. Consider how you really want parents and students to feel when they read your letter. Here's an example of what I might write for a welcome letter.

Sample Letter to Parents:

Dear Parents,

Don't you love the start of a new school year? New sneakers, fresh crayons, colorful backpacks, cool mornings at the bus stop.

There's also the flood of new worries. Will my child make friends? Will he be challenged? Will he get the support he needs in reading? What if his teacher is too strict?

Sending your kids back to school can be bittersweet. I know, I'm dealing with some of those emotions too!

I hope I can alleviate some of your worries as I send a warm welcome to another fresh school year! I'm ready to grow my next round of 5th graders and I have a feeling that you've already noticed your child taking on a bit more responsibility at home.

Each new school year brings about a new round of expectations. You and your child may already be wondering about homework, lunchtime, recess, and friendships. How about I begin by sharing a few things you can expect from me? First of all, I promise to do all I can to support, encourage, and care for your child while he/she's in my class. My top priority is connecting with students. Part of our morning routine will include something I call an "opener." Students have the opportunity to share how they're feeling, what they're worried about, and what type of support they need to be most successful each day. If a student is carrying concerns, grief, or even excitement, learning can be tricky at best. So, my plan is to make those authentic connections with students before we dig in to the academics.

Another priority is making sure that student tummies aren't growling. My own son complains that he's starving before lunch, whether I feed him a hearty breakfast or not! I know that when I'm hungry, I have trouble staying on task, so my goal is to have plenty of fruits available for students to snack on throughout our morning. I have been amazed at how readily students eat bananas, cuties, oranges, and apples. I'll be sending home a snack sign-up after the first week of school. In the past each parent has sent in a bag of fruit once a month. I also encourage students to keep a water bottle at their desks each day as hydration is crucial for brain function. We'll have recess at noon and lunch at 12:30 pm each day.

Let's see, I've addressed emotions, hunger, hydration, and recess. Next up is the friendship worry. We all want our children to have friends. Cultivating a strong classroom community is an important aspect of my role. The questions on the opener I mentioned earlier is super for helping students make connections with each other and learn empathy. I wish I could promise that your child won't experience any friendship bumps this year, though you know as well as I that life is messy. The end goal should be fostering resiliency. I can promise that I'll do my part at school to embed strategies for growing resilient kids.

Now that all the important stuff has been covered, it's time for the academic low-down. I do have high expectations for learning. I also have high expectations for myself in providing as many personalized learning opportunities as possible. I want your child to have the opportunity to learn every day- and those opportunities will look different from one student to the other. I tell lots of stories and I have a passion for engaging students in the learning process.

Homework will not feel like homework. Students are in school all day - I want them to go home and enjoy playing, sports, nature, pets, family, and hobbies. Each month students will have the opportunity to share about something they do outside of schools. I'll send home more details as to the specifics for those opportunities in a few weeks. No fretting about this! Remember my personalized learning goal? We all start from different places, so expectations for each student will look different.

Lastly, I value you - the most important people in your child's life. Please don't hesitate to email or call me with concerns, updates, or questions. We're in this together! Your child's success is just as important to me as it is to you.

There's one more thing I can promise - at some point, I'll mess up. I might misprint a date on a newsletter, not catch a spelling error on your child's essay, or even forget to respond to an email. Now, it's never my intention to make a mistake, though as human nature would have it, perfectionism won't even allow for a world without mistakes. And likewise, I can't expect you to be perfect either. I've been late to my own child's conference, forgotten to send in birthday treats, and sent my daughter to school with hives on picture day (I thought they were bug bites...)! How about we agree to offer each other some grace when it comes to these little blips?

I can't wait to meet your little ray of sunshine! We're going to have a wonderful year together. Thank you for entrusting me with your child.

With appreciation,

Mrs. Molitor

"Unless commitment is made, there are only promises and hopes; but no plans."

- Peter F. Drucker, author and educator

As you reflect on your relationships with parents, consider which of the *5 Essential C's to Parent Partnerships* that are your strengths. Most importantly, in which area could you improve?

Confidence

Communication

Compassion

Collaboration

Commitment

TIME FOR TEACHERS

Part 4

8

KEYS TO EMBRACING RESILIENCY

Protecting your Heart

I'd be remiss if I didn't offer strategies for self-care. Our jobs are demanding, and not just of our time and efforts. Teaching the way I'm suggesting requires more of our heart energy, more creative thinking, more passion, and more reflection and growth.

Both my kids are in school full-time so I thought teaching 4.5 days a week would be great this year. However, I realized how much being a mom entails, both outside and inside of the school day. I had so much to do at work, and either my kids were in my classroom, I was rushing home to meet the bus, or my husband could get the kids and I could work late. By the time I got home, I was exhausted and hungry - just like my kids. I stopped planning meals. Stopped cooking as much. Exercising was out of the question. Healthy eating habits were dwindling. Patience? That was something to admire in other, *really good* mothers.

And then one day, I got home and was REALLY exhausted. I figured I'd take a sick day, maybe two. For sure I'd be ready for school the following Monday. Well, I ended up being out for three weeks! I saw two different doctors, both recommended I get checked out at the hospital. I was super exhausted - like lie on the couch all day and night exhausted. I could sit up, but my activity level was zero. Most days I wasn't helping with the kids or making meals. My husband was taking care of our two kids, two horses, two dogs, six chickens, two fish, and two cats. He was running the kids to basketball practice and Scouts. I was just keeping up with emails and trying to figure out how to get better.

I was short of breath, and my pulse oxygen would drop from 97% to 83% with a small amount of exertion. It would even drop when I was just talking. The doc at the hospital diagnosed me with asthmatic bronchitis and my family doctor recommended that I take three weeks off. He spent a good hour with me and asked about my job. I shared with him what I was doing and that I loved it. He thought I was run down and doing too much. I was spread thin. I never wanted to miss one day, and now he wanted me to miss three weeks! In my mind, I was actually thinking that with this much time at home, I could get so much more work done... I could plan lessons, write grants, schedule PD, follow-up with teachers, prepare for Invention Convention, and I would have time to make (and eat) a nutritious breakfast.

The first few days, I just needed to rest. I checked email but I also napped and lied down most of the day. I did a lot of soul searching. What was the lesson I needed to learn? It turns out there was more than one lesson waiting for me.

I had been overcommitting myself and had no time to finish what was expected, let alone add some time for me or my family. I brought my work everywhere - to gymnastics, cheerleading, even basketball games. I figured I had six solid minutes to work on stuff during halftime.

My mom came to visit and asked how on earth I was able to keep up with this pace. I proudly shared that this was my normal, and I was balancing things pretty well. She said I looked tired.

When we run at that pace, every day, we lose sight of what balance looks like. We forget what it's like to spend quality time with our kids or husband or ourselves. We lose ourselves in our work, while rationalizing that it's for a good reason. We forget that when we run out of energy, we have nothing more to give and everyone loses.

Kids need well-charged, well-rested teachers. To be the caliber of teacher you're striving to be, you need to be well cared for. It's like the car analogy. If you knew you would only have one car for your entire life, think about how particular you'd be about its maintenance! You'd want the best oil, the tires rotated, and the fluids checked regularly. You might get it washed more frequently and you'd probably not overlook any "check engine" lights that appeared. I remember my dad warning me never to run out of gas. He said, "If your car has a fuel pump, it'll burn up if you run out of gas. Then you'll have a bigger inconvenience to get that thing fixed - not to mention it could cost $300-800!" I can't remember which of my cars did have a fuel pump, though I made sure to never run out of gas. I understood the ramifications.

Here's the thing. We know we only have one body to get us through this lifetime. I'm sure some of us take better care of our cars than our bodies. I have a friend who worked with Anthem health insurance. She told me that teachers are some of the unhealthiest people they quote. Health insurance for schools tends to be more costly than the same policy for businesses.

The stress of having so many to-do's has caused anxiety, poor eating habits, fatigue, and a lack of interest in exercising. Why the heck would I want to go to the gym after school when I was on my feet all day and just want to sit down?

I found that there are a few self-care strategies that I need to make time for if I want to keep my sanity, my job, my health and my marriage. The top 5 below are my non-negotiables - these help fulfill my basic needs.

5 Keys to Support Teacher Resiliency

#1- Water Don't underestimate this one! I know it seems too simple or obvious, though when you don't have enough, it can cause big problems. Did you know our adult bodies are made of nearly two-thirds water, and that by the time you feel thirsty, you may already be dehydrated? The rule of thumb is to drink half your weight in ounces of water daily. So if you weigh 150 pounds, you should drink 75 ounces of water. Missing a glass of water each day can affect your brain function, joints, and cardiovascular system, as the blood thickens and becomes harder to circulate.

A few years ago I started drinking 24-30 ounces of water first thing every morning. I learned this trick from my beautiful friend, Ahlea Khadro. She says the morning water routine is important for a few reasons. First, when we wake, we've been without water for 8-10 hours, so hydration becomes a top priority. Second, our body cleans up while we sleep. Imagine little workers dusting, vacuuming, and taking the trash to the curb. The trash is ready for pick-up in the morning and drinking water first thing will carry out the trash. No morning water would allow the trash (toxins) to stay and accumulate in the body. Ew. Finally, when your body knows it can count on being hydrated, it can focus on other functions, like digestion and repair.

At first, I couldn't imagine drinking even 15 ounces of water first thing in the morning, so I started small. Even 4 ounces of water will give your body a head start. I worked my way up to 24 ounces, and now I listen to my body. If I'm thirsty, I'll drink upwards of 30 ounces. If it feels like I'm forcing the water, then I know I've had enough for now.

This habit is one that's stuck. Now when I travel, I always plan to have a way of drinking a good 24-30 ounces in the morning. I crave it.

Note: No other liquids replace water. Coconut water is a great hydration drink, though even that doesn't replace water.

#2- Movement I'm not a huge fan of exercising, especially walking on treadmills or riding stationary bikes. I found that yoga is my thing, especially during the winter months. I feel calmer and stronger when I do yoga regularly - even just a couple twenty minute sessions each week. The key for me was going to a class once a week (taught by a former fabulous classroom teacher!). I found a great yoga channel on Youtube that gets me through the rest of the week. There are options for every type of yoga you might need, like sick day yoga, core strength, flexibility, sleep, and stress relief and a whole range of minutes, from 8 minutes to 75 minutes. When I feel like I just don't have the time for it, I think, "Do I really not have 10 minutes to spare to keep myself healthy?"

I live in Ohio, where the winter tends to be dreary and bleak. When April arrives, I take my movement practice outdoors as I go for walks with my kids and spend as much time outside as I can.

I'm not a jogger by any means, though I found that as I build up my stamina, even by walking, I crave movement! I'm in my early 40s and decided I needed more of a challenge in my one to three mile walks, so I added in some steep hills. I feel so good when I'm finished, proud that I exercised and my body feels stronger (and I don't feel so bad having eaten the four leftover mini-cupcakes from my daughter's birthday after school...).

Think about a stagnant pond, the kind of small pond that has so much scum on top you could almost walk across it. The water doesn't move through it and becomes thick with algae that block the sun from getting through to the water. One How-To website article, "How to Get Rid of Pond Scum," suggests that excessive algae growth is a "sign of significant nutrient imbalances."

However, simply throwing nutrients into the pond isn't enough to revive the livelihood of the pond. The scum needs to move; it literally needs to be scooped off. Our bodies are much the same. If we stay put too long, we become stagnant. Creativity won't be able to get through and likely there will be some nutrient imbalances. Movement encourages movement. Our blood flows better, our energy flows better, our life flows better.

You know the types of activities you enjoy. Light exercise will get your blood flowing and the accumulation of all the thinking on your feet and answering all the questions can move out to make room for good energy, conversation, and a feeling of peace. It feels good to let those negative things go.

#3- Sleep I include sleep at the risk of sounding like your family doctor (eat more veggies, drink more water, get eight hours of sleep). I tell my husband that sleep is more important to me than washing the dishes after dinner. I let a few housekeeping things go in an effort to attain at least seven hours of sleep. Seven is my magic number. I write myself a little to-do list on a post-note most evenings. I'll list the specifics like, go for a walk, sit in the sauna, shower, pack lunches, write, etc. It helps me prioritize what needs to be done before bedtime and if it's 10pm and the sauna is what's left, I'll aim for that the following night.

#4- **Scheduling** There are two parts to my scheduling habits that help me stay focused and get quite a bit accomplished. The first is a scheduling strategy I started doing when I was in college. Since my schedule was different everyday, I literally wrote activities from sunup to sundown and enjoyed crossing them off my list. On an ordinary day, my planner (or a post-it in my planner) might have looked like this:

8-9:15am - Class

9:15-10:30am - study for test

10:30-10:45 - head to barn

10:45-12:00 - equestrian team lesson

12-1:30pm - lunch

1:30-2pm - library- work on research paper

2-3:15pm - class

3:15- 5pm - homework, snack, clean fish tank

5-6pm - dinner with my roomie

6-7pm - OCTM meeting

7-8pm - pack for upcoming horse show

8-9pm - tv with my roomies

I actually scheduled time for studying, going to the library, cleaning my fish tank, and getting clothes ready for a horse show. Those are all things that I wouldn't write on my calendar, but since I planned for them ahead of time, they all got done. Marie Forleo says, "If it's not scheduled, it's not real." When I started out drinking water in the morning, I wrote it down on my daily schedule. If I didn't, I wouldn't remember to drink the water.

The second part to my scheduling, and how I keep track of all the pieces of my life, is a running to-do list each week. I might write things like: reschedule dentist appointment, email Carl's mom, send out 4th grade update, submit speaking proposal, make cupcakes for CC's b-day. If during the week I have a few minutes with nothing planned, I either can check my to-do list or I remember some of those important tasks and I get one accomplished. When my to-do list becomes really lengthy, I'll actually plug in some of those tasks to a spot in my week where I would make the time to do them. Doing my taxes is an item that stays on my to-do list for months... Not all my strategies are perfect. I'm definitely open to learning a better way of getting those darn taxes done!

Even now that I'm grown up and I've been teaching for 18 years, I still plan my days. When I say "plan," I don't mean lesson plans or plan the schedule for the day; those are already established. I'm talking about planning those activities into my day that aren't already part of my daily schedule. For example, yoga. I love doing yoga but it's not part of my everyday routine. Yoga is something I need to include in my weekly plan, or it doesn't get done.

So when planning for my week, I think about the activities I want to accomplish outside of my normal routine (like eating breakfast, feeding the dogs, packing lunches, etc.), and I add them to my weekly calendar. I might add yoga Monday and Thursday nights, go for a walk on Wednesday since it's supposed to be nice weather, write my book on every day except Friday, and work on my graduate homework on Thursday.

"Every minute you spend in planning saves 10 minutes in execution; this gives you a 1,000 percent return on energy!" *-Brian Tracy, author and motivational speaker*

We have a lot on our plates, both at school and at home. According to an excerpt from *The Complete Idiot's Guide to Success as a Teacher* © 2005 by Anthony D. Fredericks, "The average classroom teacher will make more than 1,500 educational decisions every school day." That's crazy! Can you imagine how many more decisions you have to make when you get home and how that number exponentially increases if you have your own children?!

If we don't prioritize and schedule self-care needs, they won't happen. You might realize that there's just not enough time for everything. That's a great place to start. What could you let go of? (Sleep cannot be an answer.)

#5- Refueling Inspiration

What inspires you? What really gets you excited about teaching? I love attending conferences, and even if I leave feeling a little overwhelmed, I always have some awesome takeaways that I implement. I usually think of ideas while I'm driving and I've been known to pull out a notepad and jot down my ideas at red lights. I found that I also get ideas when I'm out in nature.

The other day, I took my kids to a nearby creek that has lots of beachy sand. The kids made holes in the sand while I looked for colorful rocks or fossils. I started making a pile of unique rocks and wondered where the dark greens came from. I found a few fossils and wondered what the journey had been like for the organism in the fossil. I started planning an inquiry for my students.

I'd place piles of rocks from Todd's Fork Creek (that's our little nearby creek) on each table and ask students to find one that speaks to them. Then I remembered a book called Everybody Needs a Rock by Byrd Baylor - I'd read that as the students held onto their special rocks. I'd show them a map of our area of town where I found the rocks in the creek as well as a larger map of Ohio so they could get a sense of from where the rocks could have washed downstream. My question to students would be, "What journey did that rock take to make it into your hands? How long did it take?" Students can document their rock's journey, perhaps from the rock's perspective, including details about where it originated from and what historical events may have caused the rock to become the shape and size it is today. I love offering students the choice as to how they fulfill the requirements of the project. They could write a basic narrative, film a documentary, write a nonfiction book, create pretend interviews with scientists, or share as a breaking news report on tv.

I tried out the lesson with some 4th and 5th graders and the minute I placed the rocks in front of the kids, they were hooked. They were intrigued with the map of the creek and researching which type of rock they picked. One student had to leave school early, and he asked to bring his rock home with him. Another student asked if they would have time to work on this activity the following week because he enjoyed it so much. Since there was so much interest, I decided to expand the lesson. I thought I'd reach out to a local geologist and ask the students what type of product we could create to share our new knowledge - maybe something to share with our local parks.

We wrapped up our impromptu rocks exploration at the end of the year with a "one word" activity. Students chose a rock they'd like to keep and one word they'd like to take with them at the end of the year. They painted the word on their rock and took it home as a memento of our year together.

While the freedom is fun, it's also important to offer specific criteria for what's expected in the final product. This is where teachers can tailor the activity to their standards. Here's the list of standards that I would expect to develop in the rock exploration activities with a 4th grade group.

CCSS.ELA-LITERACY.W.4.3

Write narratives to develop real or imagined experiences or events using effective technique, descriptive details, and clear event sequences.

CCSS.ELA-LITERACY.W.4.3.A

Orient the reader by establishing a situation and introducing a narrator and/or characters; organize an event sequence that unfolds naturally.

CCSS.ELA-LITERACY.W.4.3.B

Use dialogue and description to develop experiences and events or show the responses of characters to situations.

CCSS.ELA-LITERACY.W.4.3.C

Use a variety of transitional words and phrases to manage the sequence of events.

CCSS.ELA-LITERACY.W.4.3.D

Use concrete words and phrases and sensory details to convey experiences and events precisely.

CCSS.ELA-LITERACY.W.4.7

Conduct short research projects that build knowledge through investigation of different aspects of a topic.

CCSS.ELA-LITERACY.W.4.8

Recall relevant information from experiences or gather relevant information from print and digital sources; take notes and categorize information, and provide a list of sources.

You know what else inspires the heck out of me? Being immersed in innovative educational environments. Sometimes it's listening to a podcast (Shout out to Danny "Sunshine" Bauer of the Better Leaders Better Schools Podcast), reading a great book (The Wild Card or 14 Things Great Teachers Do), attending a training (*The Grid Method* by the Teach Better Team has me fired up right now), listening to a great Ted Talk or keynote (Angela Maiers and Michael Bonner are both incredible!), or observing an innovative learning space.

If I were telling you about my visit to the Global Impact Stem Academy (GISA) in Springfield, Ohio via email or text, I'd be filling it with emojis! My innovation team (coined during our visit that left us feeling quite inspired) had the great fortune of going on a tour with high school principal, Michael Payne. The person who was supposed to take us on a tour wasn't available, so Michael offered. The leader of the high school dropped what he was doing at a moment's notice to take seven random educators around his school on a one-hour tour. We didn't know how lucky we were!

Michael is an incredibly authentic, passionate, dedicated educator who challenges traditional schooling by listening to students and never saying "no." His philosophy is to respond to ideas and questions by asking, "Yes, how?" Even to really bad ideas! His goal is to let his students and staff think out the solutions to determine how the solutions could work, and if they won't, they'll figure out if the solution is doable on their own instead of being shot down by him.

I've also learned to support collaboration by responding with "Yes, and..." instead of "Yes, but..." For example, a colleague shares a new idea she read on a blog - providing a brand new book for each student on the first day of school. Her colleague responds, "Yes, but we have 90 students and finding 90 donors would take all summer. What if we only got 80, would we have to buy the other 10? I really don't feel like spending any more of my money on school stuff." How did that feel to read the response? Many teachers would feel that their idea wouldn't work or isn't solid enough to pursue. Others might consider stopping all sharing of new ideas. Some might try the idea anyway, either to prove the colleague wrong, or just because it was a really good idea and now it seems a bigger challenge.

On the flip side, the response might be, "Yes, and we could create a Donor's Choose project and ask the PTO if they'd be interested in contributing a few books. We could even do a new book drive to wrap up this school year!" That felt different, didn't it? Changing one word makes a big difference. Using the word "and" elicits solutions, hope, and collaboration.

So, back to GISA, our one-hour tour lasted two and a half hours and left the seven of us brimming with new ideas for our school. We all have seven distinct personalities and experiences, ranging from 3 years experience to 22 years. Two are administrators, one parent, one self-contained fifth grade teacher, one fourth grade math teacher, one 8th grade math teacher, and me (at the time, a gifted intervention specialist and instructional coach). We were all able to get some major takeaways from our visit.

With the burden of so many of us experiencing traditional schooling (students sit obediently and accept the information delivered) and the education system organized in a way that perpetuates this traditional model, it takes many passionate, gritty professionals to persevere in finding alternative methods for teaching students to be thinkers.

GISA IS REINVENTING education for its students. Their teachers still teach standards, take state testing, get evaluated, and have the same issues with students (vaping, expulsions, etc.). Their teachers work incredibly hard and choose to work at this school to be a part of the innovation - not because the job is less intense or any easier. If anything, the job demands constant out-of-the-box thinking, and they are typically on one-year contracts. Alvin Toffler says it nicely, "The illiterate of the 21st century will not be those who cannot read and write, but those who cannot learn, unlearn, and relearn."

Lesson plans for authentic problem-based learning aren't readily available... and they *shouldn't* be. That's why it's so difficult to implement! Problem-based (or project-based) learning is an authentic, integrative approach to guiding students through the problem-solving process, a process that requires a real-life problem for students to solve. So if your school isn't going to add a new playground, taking your students through a PBL lesson to design the safest, most fun playground wouldn't be as effective or as impactful for students, or your school. The goal of PBL is to embed academics in a real-life problem that students actually find a solution for - their contribution makes an impact. There are so many PBL labeled activities that just don't fit the bill. To give the above example some credit, students would be more eager to use geometry skills to design a new playground than to calculate area and perimeter on a worksheet. So it's a step in the right direction.

There are two major expectations for the teachers at GISA: 1) to unconditionally love all the students - not just surface level rapport, but really loving the students regardless of whether or not they are "good students," turn in homework, and follow directions daily, and 2) to be messy - not by leaving paint on the tables and garbage on the floor, messy as in you're not sure where the project will take you. Students are scattered around working on different elements of the project. The classroom is noisy, the kids are active, and there may be students working on a solution that you know is totally incorrect. Your lesson plans are just outlines of the week's activities, and not because you're a slacker! There's no way to know where the learning will go. Since students are primarily driving the direction of the learning, it's tricky to plan out each day with the specifics.

On the way out, one teacher leaned in and said, "I'm thinking about putting in my resume for this place. Having that guy as an administrator would be awesome."

I nodded, "It would be cool to work here. Though guess what? Your new position for next year (makerspace and career exploration) already lands you a new administrator and he's giving you full flexibility to be as innovative as you want."

Think about it. Our little team of administrators, teachers, and a parent were all inspired by this new approach to school. We all listened intently as the passionate principal shared his philosophy of education and the innovative ways his school was defining teaching. To inspire seven very different educators is quite the feat.

Dylan Wiliam, from the University of London, sums it up well:

If we create a culture where every teacher believes they need to improve, not because they are not good enough, but because they can be even better, there is no limit to what we can achieve.

Yes! That culture.

Here's something else I realized. We may all feel moved by those youtube videos where a teacher sees beyond a misbehaving student and provides encouragement and support so that the student finally ends up learning to read. Years later, the student realizes that the teacher changed his life. Or we hear a motivational speaker and think, "Yes! That! I totally believe it. I can make a difference!"

However, as we head back to school and reality sets in, we discover that the inspiration we felt is swiftly swept away by the day-to-day demands of teaching. We're grading, copying, planning, and getting homework ready. The overwhelming exhaustion, lack of sleep, and fatigue return. Yes, we still love our students, though making time to let that inspiration grow and develop into something new doesn't happen like we envisioned. The old habits return and that brief feeling of inspiration is swiftly carried away by the mediocrities of teaching.

Growing professionally will happen faster and more effectively if we also grow personally. When I started getting into the research around standards-based grading, I discovered that the traditional mindset around grading student work also needed to shift. And when I started supporting my colleagues with the shift, I realized the enormity of that shift. We've been ingrained in traditional schooling our whole lives, and our parents before us. A means good student, B means average, C means just ok, D means bad student, and F is worse.

Some of the common complaints about standards-based grading

include: what to do when a student doesn't turn in an assignment, how do we communicate to parents that a 3 (on a 4-point scale) is exactly where the student should be, what will colleges do with 3s and 4s vs. As and Bs, and how do students show they are exceeding standards.

Getting the answers to some of these questions may require a shift away from traditional thinking, or at least a willingness to see a different perspective.

Think about something you've implemented in your classroom for years. It could be checking fluency, daily math warm-ups, homework, incorporating neatness into a math or reading project grade, or weekly spelling tests. Could you defend that practice in a way that would get people to stand up and applaud? Sometimes we stick to teaching practices because they're comfortable or we've done them for years and they seem to work. Sometimes for us to grow, to really stretch ourselves, we need to let go of our old standbys. Don't we ask the same of our students?

Inspiration fuels innovation. I'm more likely to push myself, try something new, stumble on an awesome lesson if I'm inspired. Eleanor Roosevelt said, "Do one thing every day that scares you." For some of us, this might be trying flexible seating. For others, it might be revisiting weekly spelling tests. What's the first thing that comes to your mind when you think of a change in your classroom or instructional practices that scares you? That. Do that.

Self-Care Exercise:

Let's figure out what you need to stay energized, fresh, and inspired. Get out a notebook and either journal this question or create a mindmap. Write "The Best Me" in the middle and then brainstorm all the self-care, inspiring, restful activities that you need to be the best you (as a teacher, wife, husband, mom, sister, daughter, etc.). Then pick the top three and schedule those. Once those become a routine, choose a few more and schedule those.

Why Evaluations Ruin Your Day (or month...)

Does preparing for your evaluation take countless hours? You search for just the right lesson, one that matches your pacing guide for the unit on the day your administrator is scheduled to observe. You spend time writing an extensive three page lesson plan (just like you always do...), remember to incorporate some level of differentiation, include a few really great questions, and get all your copies and materials together. Sigh.

Oh wait, then you need to prepare for the preconference, so you answer all of those questions, which then prompts you to revise your lesson plans a bit. After all that planning, you're now ready to give up your plan time to have a preconference and finally the day of the evaluation arrives. You've given your students a friendly reminder (some might use the word "threat") to be on their best behavior, and as soon as the administrator walks in, your heart rate quickens, you notice your speech is slightly shaky, and you feel more nervous than you thought you would. You try not to notice as the administrator types away and peers over students' shoulders. You pray that she questions the students who will give the best answers.

As soon as the admin leaves, you take a deep breath and become normal again. Over lunch, you find yourself reflecting on the pacing of the lesson, and you already have three things you would change if you could do the lesson over again.

The next few days you carry a slight anxiety around as you contemplate the outcome of your observation. You're not really worried about being fired, but you want to be stellar. You want to be a shining star of a teacher. You want confirmation that you're an accomplished teacher, something to recognize all those long hours planning, grading, and communicating with parents.

The next step is planning the post-conference during another plan time, to review your lesson and give you a final score or rating. Nerves creep back, you're armed with your reflection, and you're feeling a little apprehensive. What if she didn't like my lesson? What if she thought the pacing was too quick? What if she realizes my teaching isn't that great? You wish the administrator could have seen how you wrapped up the lesson because students were sharing such great connections and ah-ha moments.

And somewhere, a hint of defensiveness slinks its way in.

The post-conference goes well, overall. There are a few areas of recommendation, which is a little disappointing considering all the time spent pouring ideas into the planning. You wanted a perfect score. You work hard and you know you're a good teacher, it's nice to have that validation. Instead, you feel criticized and you may even find yourself slightly hating the administrator.

This adds up and contributes to a layer of stress that you don't need.

So, how do we overcome the stress from teacher evaluations?

First, it's important that you understand where this anxiety and defensiveness comes from. It turns out that we are hard-wired to seek out or look for threats. Tim Kight, of the Focus 3 Podcast, says that there's such a thing as negativity bias; "It's easy find, fixate and focus on things that are negative." It's our body's way of managing risk, though in this day and age, our body is perceiving judgements and non-threatening comments as harmful. Brian Kight says, "You're going to get triggered, biologically, by something that feels or looks like a threat, that really isn't." So a big part of our initial response is due to our body's perception of a threat - a threat to our well-being, our job, our status.

Defensiveness, then, seems to stem from fear. With this understanding, we can pause when we feel ourselves bracing after criticism, regardless of how constructive it may be.

Brian Kight offers really great advice for how to deal with feedback or criticism.

1- Is it true?

Consider this. The principal asks to chat with you about a parent email, and immediately you feel yourself bracing, and getting defensive. One of your student's parents emailed the principal, explaining that her daughter is having trouble with a few friends at lunch and in the hallway after recess. The principal wants to meet with you to see what's going on.

Instead of reacting, "Why didn't the mom email me? Why didn't the daughter come to me with her concerns? Is the principal upset with me?," you might first consider, "Is it true?" Does the girl have problems with anyone in the hallway? Have you noticed anything at lunch?

2- What was the intent of the person sharing?

Why is the principal asking you? Why did the parent email the principal? If we reflect and consider their reasons for reaching out, perhaps they are looking out for the best interest of the student. The parent might think that since the issues are happening outside the classroom that it would be best to contact the principal. The principal knows it's best to get the scoop from the person who knows the student best. No part of the situation is threatening, though there's a part of us that perceives it as just that.

Here's another example. I was reviewing word forms in a 3rd grade classroom and the word was "order." Students were sharing other forms of the word: reorder, ordering, ordered, orders, when a parent volunteer (who had a history of being negative and demanding) walks in my room to get a stapler. She catches on to what we're doing and says over her shoulder as she walks out, "How about 'disorder?' I'm sure you see that a lot."

This was my 2nd year teaching, and I was instantly offended and upset. But had I stopped to consider if her comment was true, I could have avoided some misery. No, thinking about my students and the physicality of my classroom, I never considered there to be disorder. And, had I considered her intent, I would have realized that this was either supposed to be deemed funny, or she was trying to offend me. Either way, there was no need to stay offended or upset.

We're also wired to look for opportunity. Ann Marie writes in her blog *We're Wired To Connect And Protect,* our brains "track for perceived threats to our physical safety, but also for threats to our sense of belonging, self-image, or emotional integrity. The most innocuous instances, like someone vocalizing an opinion opposite to ours, can threaten our sense of stability, security, or worth." Inevitably, we're going to be triggered emotionally by something we perceive as a threat, though the opportunity to learn how to navigate those triggers can be the catalyst for life-changing growth.

Anne Marie continues,

One of the ultimate human paradoxes is that we long for connection and yet we automatically protect ourselves for fear of being hurt, abandoned, betrayed, or rejected. Our primal nature is messy and wild. One minute we feel connected, the next moment we might be opposing, judging, defending, blaming and protecting. Transformation begins when we're honest about our reactivity. Our medicine is to bring humor and compassion to these primal parts, individually and collectively.

Where do we go from here?

Congratulations! You stuck with me, you finished. I hope you've made some great connections, had several awesome ideas, and you now feel something stirring inside you. Let those stirring emotions and ideas guide you. Step outside your comfort zone, you might shine there! Take a risk. Be the teacher you may be hiding within. But above all, follow your heart.

Professional development can be really helpful, and authentic, meaningful, heart-based **personal** development is the jet fuel that can propel you to being the teacher of the year - maybe not in an award recognized by the state, but by your students, parents, and the community.

Stretch yourself. Grow. Support your colleagues. Love. Ask. Get curious.

Take this fire in your belly and use it to fuel the transformation you feel brewing. You might create a quick mind map of to organize all your new ideas. Grab a sheet of paper and draw a bubble in the middle - you could call it "My Teaching Transformation." Jot down all the big ideas you're thinking about (differentiation, writing your vision, heart-based teaching, questions, stories, R.A.C.E., parent rapport). Once you've written out all the big ideas, go back under each idea and reference a page number, a quote, or a few words to remind you what you could do. Add color and pictures and either slip it in a page protector, or slip it in the front of a clear binder. Use this map as a guide for your school year.

We don't need to sit back and wait for policy-makers to change education. We are teachers. We have the power to transform education! What do you say? I know teaching is overwhelming, keeping up with the ever-changing demands is stressful, evaluations can take the wind out of your sails, and grading papers keeps you from sleeping. I also know this: Your circumstances don't define you, nor the teacher you're meant to be. You've got this. I believe in you.

Even with new state mandates, piles of grading, meetings, and seemingly small amounts of plan time, **you still have the power in the classroom to teach from your heart, to teach with the talents you already possess, and to see the gifts every day brings.**

After all, we teach *children*, not curriculum.

RESOURCES

R.A.C.E. Checklist

Simply copy this and cut into slips to tape in your planner. Or, make your own labels that stick right into your lesson planner!

Learning Target:

Relevancy:
Attention Grabber aka "The Hook":
Challenging Question:
Emotion evoked by:

This is for you if you're...

- Ready to speed up your lesson planning process
- Unclear and feeling stuck about how to engage students better with the weight of the hefty state standards
- Struggling to keep your head above water and losing interest in teaching, and
- Committed to making a bigger impact while enjoying the inspiring teaching career you envisioned years ago.

Lesson planning lays the foundation of your day - it's how students both learn from and connect with you. Having a well thought-out action plan for the day, one that will engage students, can give you a boost of confidence and peace of mind. Not to mention, a well-organized, engaging lesson gives students choice, challenges, and coaching opportunities.

10-Minute Lesson Plan Template

Writing a lesson can take minutes instead of hours. Your students are going to love the engaging lingo, and you'll get excited and feel re-inspired to teach. Yay!!! Let's get started...

Step 1: Upgrade your Learning Target

Choose an "*I Can*" statement and give it some flair! Aim for something clear, specific, and relevant to the kids to authentically get their attention. Incorporating alliteration can make your target stronger. You'll see from the examples below that the learning target can become the challenging question. Relevancy, attention grabbing, and challenge all in one sentence! The more you work with the examples below, the better and quicker you'll be. Plus, this can be such a fun step!

Instead of creating your own right away, simply switch out the underlined topics for your ideas:

How can you Multiply Decimals so you can calculate sales tax on a brand new car?

Is it possible to become a Master Multiplier in the next 5 days?

Learn how to run for U.S. President in 5 Simple Steps.

Learn 5 ways to solve a word problem so you can help a famous King solve a problem.

What are the 3 Top Secrets to Figuring out New Words?

Step 2: Plan the Lesson

Plot out the 3 main steps in delivering the lesson. This box may take the most time to complete as it's the bulk of your lesson.

1. Mini-lesson: Engage and evoke emotion. Read a book, tell a story about you, play a song, show a video clip, share a mystery, or pose a problem.
2. Practice: How will students try it out? What will students

need to do to show proficiency? Choice boards or menus can support students at any level! It's important to offer choice and make the assignment relevant here too.

3. Extension: How can students investigate deeper? As soon as students show competency, you can move them on to the extensions. Remember: Not more of the same, but more in depth.

Step 3: Wrap-up

Evaluate what they've learned. Lots of ideas here, just circle one!

- Summarize their learning in a 2-minute skit
- Write a news story spotlighting the amazing learning today
- Create an assessment or learning opportunity for their peers
- Create an info postcard-picture with example on front, details on back
- Letter to a friend explaining "How to run for President in 5 simple steps"
- Testimonial - "Three top secrets for finding out new words" worked for me! Here's how.
- Exit card that revisits Learning Target:
- Is it possible to become a Master Multiplier in the next 5 days? Explain and give examples.
- *Based on your learning today, what do you think will be the next steps tomorrow?*
- Write an ad to highlight their understanding of objective: *How to Multiply in 3 Easy Steps*
- Create a slideshow to show "How to Multiply Decimals to calculate sales tax on a brand new car"
- Use mini-lesson discoveries as questions: *How do you...? What is the biggest challenge you faced...? What is the most powerful secret to...?*

10- Minute Lesson Plan Template

Step 1: Upgrade your Learning Target

Learn how to _________ so you can _____________.

Learn how you can be a _______ in the next ________.

Learn how to ______________ in ___________ steps.

Learn ___ ways to _______ so you can ___________.

Learn ___ Top Secrets to _______________________.

____

____

Step 2: Plan the Lesson

1. **Mini-lesson:** tell a story song video clip book mystery problem _________________ (other)

2. **Practice**: Choice & Relevant

What will students need to do to show proficiency?

What can I offer students who are struggling? manipulative chunk assignment

3. **Extension:** How can students investigate deeper? Bloom's Taxonomy

Step 3: Wrap-up: How will they show what they learned?

Ask students: On a scale from 1-10 (best ever), how fun was this lesson? ______
What was the most important concept you learned?

Evaluate:

- How fun was this lesson for you? On a scale from 1-10 (best ever!) _____
- How effective was this lesson (What % mastered the target)? ______

Make revisions based on your evaluation and student feedback.

Quick Notes Home

- Edwin brings such a positive energy to our classroom! Thanks for sharing him with us.
- Cecelia is quite the helper. She's always the first to lend a hand.
- Edwin has the best sense of humor! I can count on him to chuckle at all my jokes.
- Cecelia is growing so much. It's great to see her confidence bloom!
- Edwin has been a wonderful friend. He seems to know who needs a smile at just the right time.
- I'm blown away by Cecelia's artistic abilities! She shared her princess drawing this week and all the students clapped for her.
- Edwin is a voracious reader! He always keeps a stockpile of

about 15 books nearby so that he's never without a good book. I love his passion! Now if I can just get him to lunch without bringing a few books. :)

- Cecelia sets high standards for herself. It's fun to watch her celebrate reaching her reading goal!
- Edwin has been an essential tech helper this week. He's great at troubleshooting computer issues and getting student computers up and running.
- Cecelia has been sharing all about her new pony. Would you like to send a picture so she can show the class?
- Edwin loves a challenge! I'm thrilled that he seeks out opportunities to grow his brain.
- I discovered that Cecelia enjoys leading the class in a few yoga poses. I see a future teacher!
- Edwin is the most polite student! He says please and thank you every day, even when I pass out a test!
- I appreciate Cecelia's smile every morning. She seems to bring happiness with her every day!
- Edwin has been working so hard this week! We started a new project and he jumped right in.
- Cecelia is like a little ray of sunshine! She shines so brightly that she lifts other students up.
- Edwin has the best jokes. I can count on him when I need a good chuckle. :)
- Cecelia asks the best questions! Her curiosity inspires the other students.
- I've been watching Edwin's leadership skills grow this year. I expect to hear about his big accomplishments in the future.

Opener and Closer

Name ______________________________

Class Warm-up

What are you **bringing** with you today?	What support do you need today to be your **best**?	What are you ready to **let go** of today or what have you been struggling with?
What has gone **well** for you this week?	What is one thing you can do today that you'll be **proud** of?	Sit for a few moments & **visualize** how you'd like today to go. Get specific with how you want to feel, act, and achieve.

Closing

What are you **taking** with you today?	Write **one word** that sums up today.	What are you beginning to **notice**, **realize**, or **understand** after today's class?
What was the **best** thing about today?	What is one thing you did today that you are **proud** of?	What are you **grateful** for?

ABOUT THE AUTHOR

Jen is a Master Teacher, motivational speaker, and author of The Happy Teacher's Handbook. Her superpower is getting teachers to smile again. She brings a refreshing perspective that lifts you up when you want to walk out, reminding you of the real reason you became a teacher.

She has this amazing ability to shift perspective from the overwhelm of state mandates to the fire within you that keeps you going.

She reminds you that you still have power in the classroom to teach from your heart, to teach with the talents you already possess, and to see the gifts every day brings.

You'll finish this book feeling inspired, more focused and more capable of managing your time. You'll be able to prioritize what really matters and get back to the heart of teaching.

As an elementary teacher of 18 years, Jen has enjoyed teaching in the classroom, as a gifted intervention specialist, and more recently as an instructional coach. She has presented to leadership teams, school board members, regional meetings, national conferences, local businesses, parent groups, and in front of the Ohio State Superintendent.

www.happyteachershandbook.com

SMILES ARE CONTAGIOUS!

Thank you for reading my book!

I really appreciate all of your feedback, and I love hearing what you have to say. Please leave a helpful review on Amazon.

I need your input to make the next version of this book and my future books even better. I believe we're overdue for an overhaul of traditional education. Students deserve to learn and think at every age. Teachers deserve the training, resources, and time to implement this overhaul. Schools should prepare students for careers that fuel the spark in their hearts, not careers that just pays the bills.

Teachers inspired by this book will become change-makers in their own classrooms. The more teachers who cultivate these the changes, the more students who will benefit. This is how we change education.

Please join me on FB @TheHappyTeachersBook to get free resources and sneak peaks of my new books.

Thank you for teaching. Thank you for loving your students and putting in all those extra hours to make a bigger impact.

To Happy, Resilient Teaching!
Jen Molitor

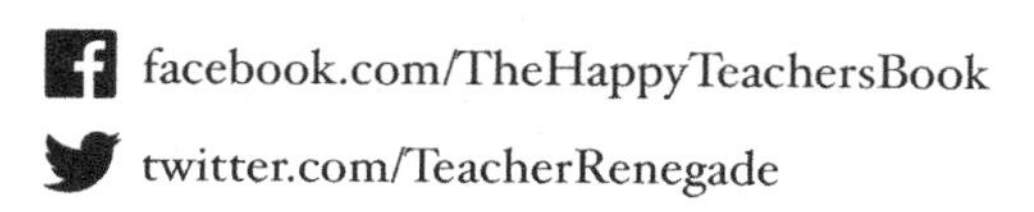

Made in the USA
Monee, IL
25 June 2021